THE MODERN MONEY MANIFESTO

THE MODERN MONEY MANIFESTO

The No-Nonsense Guide to Boosting Your Finances

CHARLOTTE JESSOP

First published in the UK in 2024 by Bedford Square Publishers Ltd,
London, UK

bedfordsquarepublishers.co.uk
@bedsqpublishers

A CIP catalogue record for this book is available
from the British Library.

ISBN
978-1-83501-063-1 (Trade Paperback)
978-1-83501-064-8 (eBook)

2 4 6 8 10 9 7 5 3 1

Typeset in Adobe Caslon by Palimpsest Book Production Limited,
Falkirk Stirlingshire

Printed in Great Britain by CPI Group (UK) Ltd, Croydon CR0 4YY

To Emily and Alice

Money Then and Now

Sometimes I feel like I wasted my twenties. It wasn't that I didn't have fun or achieve great things, it's just that when I look back that time of my life doesn't feel very me.

My experience is typical of my generation. In fact, I probably had the textbook definition of a good upbringing, and it screams privilege from many directions. I was raised by boomers with public sector jobs. We had a nice house, I went to a nice school, I had nice friends and was blessed with a brain that would enable me to be whatever I wanted to be when I grew up.

In fact 'you could be whatever you wanted to be' was pretty much repeated daily in my house. I believed it to an extent. Going to an all-girls' school also lit a fire in my heart that told me that I, a woman, had a duty to break through glass ceilings and pave a better future for the women who came after us.

So how on Earth did I end up a teacher, married with two kids and a three-bed end-of-terrace house in the middle of Norfolk before I'd even hit 30?

That was not what I had pictured for myself.

Granted, I'd always wanted a family and a partner that cared for me, but there was supposed to be an exciting career, travel and adventure.

What happened was I had fallen into the boomer financial advice trap.

You might be familiar with it; it goes like this:

- Work hard at school
- Get a good job
- Save
- Buy a house
- Buy a bigger house
- Retire in your early sixties with a final salary pension and, if you've worked really hard, a second home in Gran Canaria.

It is easy to see why I was seduced by this plan. It is simple and I was watching my parents execute this strategy with great success. I mean, it worked for them, so why wouldn't it work for me?

Well, it didn't. And it wasn't my fault.

For nearly three decades, I subscribed to the idea that this would work out for me. I left school with good GCSEs and A levels, went to university to study mathematics, and hoped to go on to be either an actuary or a civil engineer.

At this point, I felt kinda burnt out and, coupled with the recession that hit in 2008–09, my dreams of high-flying careers were diminishing. Desperate to salvage some of the Boomer Dream, I decided to go into teaching.

Not only did my love of numbers ooze into my teaching, but I found that I had a way with words. Explaining complicated topics in an easily digestible way came easily to me. Furthermore, I was full of ambition. Determined to make the most of the career that I had stumbled into, I applied for more and more responsibility and enjoyed the increased pay that came with it.

At this point, I had saved up for my first house with my soon-to-be husband using a combination of the money I had saved from working my butt off during university and a small golden hello that I received when I entered the teaching profession.

Sticking to the rules, I got married and then decided to have a couple of kids. This was probably the straw that broke the camel's back.

When I turned 30, I realised that my life wasn't like that of my parents. My dad worked full-time and my mum did some part-time work, but was mostly at home. For us though? Well, both my husband and I would need to work to pay the mortgage and bills. On top of that, we would have to work to pay for childcare or find some intricate system where we worked alternative shifts so that we could avoid childcare but also each other.

But this was survival. That's all that was available to us.

I didn't want to survive. I wanted to thrive.

For the first time, I took a long hard look at the Boomer Dream, and found that there was no way that it could work for me. Plus, I didn't even want it to work. I didn't want that at all. What I wanted was a career that I loved, time with my family, lots of travel, and to feel the joys of financial stability both in retirement and now. Also, I wanted to work a little less hard. Smarter? Sure. Occasionally hard? Yeah maybe. But with lots of time for rest and relaxation? Hells yes!

I know that I am not the only one who feels like this. I see this same exhaustion in the eyes of the other parents on the school run, in the group WhatsApp chats with my friends, and, sadly, I saw it in the faces of my students. They hadn't even started work but were already tired from the pressure to succeed and conform. To fulfil a destiny that wasn't designed for them.

I know you feel it too.

Enter the Modern Money Manifesto.

In the blur of sleepless nights while on maternity leave with my youngest, I desperately searched for a different way to live my life. For a set of rules that would work for me, like how the rules my parents had lived by had worked for them.

The realisation soon set in that there were no rules. The expectation was that I would live my life by those same rules, but experience worse outcomes and be miserable for most of my life. Plus, if I dared to complain that I didn't like the rules or that I wasn't able to do it any more, I would be met with an army of boomer headlines telling me that avocados were my problem. Eh? I don't even like avocados.

I needed a new set of rules. But I was going to have to make them myself.

Over the next year or so, I changed my life.

In letting go of the traditional life path, I allowed new rules to show themselves to me. I let them in and magic happened.

This is what went down:

- I started working part-time. My husband did too. Despite a significant reduction in hours, we had more disposable income than if we had both continued to work.
- I paid off chunks of my mortgage. Using some of our savings and surplus cash, we managed to halve our monthly mortgage payments.
- I started a business. With some of the additional free time I had from working part-time, I started a blog. This allowed me to develop skills that would take me away from my teaching job and to create additional income, and eventually a way for my family to escape the constraints of the nine-to-five.
- I took my family on a trip around the world. With our newfound freedom, income, time, and some deep reflection on our life goals, we said goodbye to our jobs and our house and spent seven months hopping from country to country.

The best part was that I didn't have to compromise. It doesn't need to be a choice between travel or starting a family. Buying a house or paying into a pension. I was able to find a way to do it all.

Now if you are rolling your eyes and thinking, 'Sure I could do all that if I had money too,' well, I am here to tell you that I am probably not as rich as you think. I'm certainly not a millionaire and, at the time of writing, I've not even got close to earning six figures. (Although I believe that both of these will come in time.) My husband isn't the source of my money either. He will happily tell you that I am the money-maker and I have out-earned him my entire life.

Yes, I benefit from some privileges. I am white and I am well educated. I also come from a family that has financial security. Like I said, they have achieved the ultimate boomer goals, by working hard, saving and buying increasingly bigger properties. But I'll confess that I grew up without worrying about money too much.

Working against me is my womanhood, a hearing loss that means I wear hearing aids, and the fact that somehow I have ended up living in Norfolk which is hardly a hub for career opportunities.

My point is that I'm not some trust fund baby. I am just a person with a fascination with money and dreams above her station and I found a way to make it work. Better still, I found a way to make it work for you too.

Why Should I Trust You?

Fair question! We don't know each other.

You might be one of the people who follow me on Instagram, TikTok, or YouTube, in which case, 'Hello old friend.' But if you've randomly picked up this book, then you might not know who I am or have seen one of my many post-run, make-up-down-my-face Instagram story binges where I put the world to rights on the financial issue of the day.

For you, I will start at the beginning.

I am a nerd. I've loved maths for as long as I can remember. I came pretty much top of my year group every year throughout high school, which is no mean feat in a grammar school surrounded by other super-intelligent girls. At fourteen, I decided I loved money too and opted to study an economics GCSE, which I followed with an A level. Ultimate nerd move. I continued to study mathematics because I wasn't convinced whether a career in finance or engineering was for me. To procrastinate on this decision further, I opted to study mathematics at university.

2008 landed with a bang halfway through my studies. The credit crunch and global recession saw graduate banking and finance jobs disappear almost overnight. My post-university options were narrowing and my mum told me that becoming a teacher would be a smart move. Seemingly incapable of making my own decisions, I did what she said and completed a PGCE. What followed was a ten-year career as a mathematics teacher.

Like I said, I was an ambitious young thing, so I worked hard (there it is again) to impress the bosses aka other teachers earning a tiny bit more money than me. One way I did this was to teach personal finance within my lessons. There are plenty of opportunities to do this within the maths curriculum, but there aren't many teachers who would decide to include it in their lessons. I loved it though. My students loved it even more. They enjoyed my lessons, where we would make budgets using income from real jobs that I had found online. This involved scrolling through RightMove to find the perfect house, within budget and in the right area. This sort of practical mathematics lit them up.

Eventually, I hit that wall that I told you about, the 'why tf isn't my life turning out the way my parents promised?' wall, and figured that if I was feeling this that there were thousands, if not millions, of other people out there, like you, who felt the same.

That's when I started a blog. In *Looking After Your Pennies* I chronicled my financial learning as I began to look at my finances differently and took the steps to learn more. I'm not a selfish person, so I started sharing what I knew on my website.

Now my 'blog' is seven years old and is more than just a blog. It is a YouTube channel, an Instagram account, a TikTok page, it was a podcast for a bit, and it is a community of people who are keen to learn more about their money and change their lives.

My business has caught the attention of a few people too. BBC News, Sky News, the *Sun*, Martin Lewis, the *Telegraph* and the *Financial Times*, to name a few. All begging for my opinion on the latest financial topic that was hitting the news. I've sat on the BBC red sofa and told parents how they can save money on uniform costs. I went on the *Financial Times* podcast *The Money Clinic* and talked about the importance of budgeting. And millions watched me tell Martin Lewis about the eco-friendly ways in which I saved money for my trip around the world.

Close to 100,000 people follow my social accounts to get my take on managing money, and hundreds have taken this wisdom and used it to achieve incredible outcomes in their own lives.

The same people have also been telling me over and over that I NEED to write a book, and I've procrastinated on that too. There was always something else to do, and a lovely dose of self-doubt to convince me to step away from the keyboard.

But in the current economic climate, we need a financial revolution more than ever. That all-girls'-school feminist fire in my heart burns strong with the urge to spread the word and as many people as possible to create the financial freedom that they have long desired.

What Can I Expect from This Book?

You probably picked this book up because you too have grown weary of the relentlessness of working hard to chase after things that you are not even sure you want. Last time you checked, you were heading off to university, and now it is several years later and you are still poor and even the old goals seem to get further and further out of reach.

The headlines in the newspapers about house prices, inflation and student loans have trampled your dreams into the dirt and at some point you stopped even trying to 'get ahead' and resigned yourself to a life existing.

Your hope is that this book will change that. And it will.

Your life is likely to be a lot different from your parents' and grandparents' lives. For one, you could be reading this on a mobile phone on a beach thousands of miles from home, or listening in your car on the way to bottomless brunch. Why should you expect that what worked for them is going to work for you?

Perhaps the pandemic means that you are now working entirely remotely. You may have never even met your co-workers. You might be what Emma Gannon describes as a multi-hyphenate – a person who wears many hats to make their money.

It could be that you live in an entirely different country from your family. You've taken the decision to uproot yourself and try your luck in a new city where the opportunities for your industry are abundant. Or maybe you wanted to find a community that was more your fit.

You have the opportunity for more freedom around your lifestyle than ever before. Yet the financial guidance that is found in books, podcasts, newspapers, blog posts and YouTube videos still largely speaks to the work hard, buy a house, retire mentality.

Honestly, it is boring and it keeps you small.

Like most aspects of boomer living, we are cancelling that crap. It worked for them, but you are part of the generation that is redefining finance. You are saying no to burning out. No to waiting until retirement before seeing the world. No to being like everyone else, because what you want to be is YOU.

I am your new best friend and I am here to show you how to thrive now.

How to Get the Most from This Book

Some books are read-once-and-move-on sort of books. Others become your own personal Bible that give you guidance when you are starting to doubt yourself or your actions. I like to think of this book as the latter.

Your finances are not something that you can set up, pat yourself on the back about and then ignore for the rest of your life. Unless you are a billionaire of course, but I doubt many of them need to read a book about personal finance.

Instead, you will find that your finances will change and vary over the course of your life. As will you. Therefore, coming back to good foundational practices could be key. You may think of this book as a template. When you get to a new chapter of your life, you may unlock a new section of that template and need to revert to the wisdom within these pages.

Let's look at some examples of what I am talking about.

Right now, you may be single, living on your own or with parents, with no kids, no mortgage and your number one goal is to bring the money in and enjoy your life. For you, the chapters on getting paid, tax and sorting out your spending might be of most use now.

But a couple of years down the line, you could be in a different place. Perhaps you've found the love of your life and want to find a house and start a family. You haven't forgotten about the fact that you want to enjoy life, but you have different goals and objectives now. At this stage of your life, you may want to look into whether buying a house is right for you, or ensuring that you have savings so that you can still keep those big goals in mind.

Personally, I recommend that you start by reading the whole book. You will learn something from every chapter that you can apply to all areas of your finances. Even if that particular chapter doesn't resonate with you in the present moment, you may unlock some strategies that put you in a good place when you reach that stage of your life.

To support you on your journey to a better financial future and greater freedom in your life, I have included some activities throughout the chapters. They will help you gauge where you are currently, guide you to what you need to do next, and share some tips and hints on how to stay motivated as you work on this area of your life.

This is designed to get you to take action.

Many people have big dreams for their lives. They want change, freedom or success. But they choose to live life the same as they have always done while waiting for the solution to fall out of the sky in some miraculous fashion.

The problem with that is that it takes control away from you. You are trusting someone else to find the answers and do the work. Have you ever blown the candles out on a birthday cake and wished you could win the lottery? Did you actually buy a lottery ticket that week? Therein lies the problem.

You know the change that you want but you are hoping that someone else bought the lottery ticket for you. People don't normally do that. That's a 'you' thing to do!

This book has the potential to radically alter your financial situation. It can provide clarity and understanding about how you can thrive in the current financial world. But if you read it, smile to yourself, and then do nothing, nothing will change. You will just be another person gliding along in the world of boomer rules.

Instead, you can turn the page and read the next chapter. Talk to your partner or friend about what you read. Make a promise to yourself that you will show up. Then maybe in a year or two you will be one of those people who send me DMs or emails thanking me for the difference that I have made in their lives. Not bragging, just saying.

My hope is that you read this book and find a system that enables you to financially thrive. Then together we can spread the word and help more people achieve their goals. This isn't a selfish mission. It is meant to be shared. You and I have lived too long within a financial framework that doesn't work for us. It is time to throw out that framework. Tear up the rulebook. Ignore the financial advice of old.

It is time for a financial revolution.

Chapter One

Cut Yourself Some Slack

> 'When I bought my first property, going abroad, the easyJet, gym, Netflix lifestyle didn't exist!' Kirstie Allsopp (clueless TV person)

These sorts of comments have been near-constant since millennials came of age. Essentially, the older generations created a load of technology that made our lives easier and more exciting, then criticised us when we used it.

You have probably seen the many complaints about the over-consumption of avocado toast and chai lattes that are used to explain why our lives are not conforming to THEIR version of what we should achieve.

The problem is that you have been told you should want what they think you should want so many times that you actually want it yourself now. But the world that you live in is nothing like the world that your parents and grandparents grew up in. I mean back in their day it was just toast and coffee for one thing.

With this new world of opportunities, why does it feel harder than ever to thrive?

The reason is that it IS harder.

What the Hell Is Going On with Housing?

Let's assume for a second that deep in your heart you long to buy your first property. You have dreams of one day owning a cottage with a river that runs through the back garden, and getting that little flat close to work is the first foot on that ladder and one small step closer to that dream.

Buying property is a national obsession in the UK. As soon as you hit your twenties, someone will ask you at least once a week if you have bought a house yet. It is low-level indoctrination and, even if you want to spend your life checking out the world's top surfing spots, eventually you will succumb and start saving to get your foot on the first rung. But more on that in Chapter Six.

Back in the eighties, the average house sold for around £19,000, with the average salary sitting at £6,000. It is hard to imagine that it was possible to live on such a small income, but the price of many other daily essentials was lower too.

Fast-forward to today and the average salary sits at around £30,000, but the average property price is £274,000. This is over nine times the average salary. Back in the eighties average property prices were around three times the typical yearly wage. Therefore buying houses is more expensive now.

I remember scoffing at my parents when they told me how little they had paid for their first house. They did a lot of backtracking about how my dad's wage was only £10 a week at that point so it was all relative. At the time, I believed that, and kept my thoughts about how I wished they'd bought a couple more houses at those prices to myself.

It wasn't until I was talking to my dad about how I was proud of my husband and me for paying off significant amounts of our mortgage that I realised the true extent of how my parents had lucked out with the housing market.

When I said that we only had £85,000 left to pay on our mortgage, he piped up with, 'I don't think our mortgage was ever more than £60k.' This was when I saw the reality of the situation, as their house now is worth more than double, probably close to triple, what my house is worth. On top of that, it wasn't that long ago that they finished paying the mortgage off. I'm not bitter. If anything, I'm jealous. But more understanding by our boomer relatives of the realities of homeowners in the present would be appreciated.

Your Savings Aren't All Right

House prices are just one area that has changed dramatically. Savings are another where it has become harder for younger generations to thrive. Interest rates on savings have never been known for being great at generating a healthy return on your cash but, as a minimum, you hope that you might earn enough to combat the effects of inflation.

This held true for most of the eighties, nineties, and even the early noughties, when average savings account interest rates beat, or as a minimum matched, the rate of inflation.[1] However, since the 2008–09 recession, there have only been two years when this has been true. Thanks 2014 and 2015.

For our parents, saving meant that their money would at least, in some way, be working for them. It would earn interest and, when they came to spend it, it would be able to buy them roughly the same amount of stuff as when they first saved it.

In the last ten years though, if you have been putting your money in a savings account, the chances are that you will now have less money in real terms. Prices have gone up by more than your savings. It is now harder to save money than it has been for the previous 30 years. Yet you still need to have some savings. The downside is that you have to sit and watch it lose value, while waiting for your washing machine to explode or some other emergency that you need that money for.

Alas, it doesn't stop there.

Investing is one way to attempt to get a better return on your hard-earned cash. But even that is not as good as it once was – or at least that has been the trend over the last few years.

Let's take for example the S&P 500. This is the top 500 companies in the US, but I'll explain more about that in Chapter Ten where I'll give you all the ins and outs of investing. For now, though, I want to look at what would have happened if you had invested in these 500 companies between 1980 and 2000.

Well, the result would have been an average annual return of 16.22 per cent. Yep! That's a lot more than that money would have made sitting in ANY bank account. Obviously, some years were better than others, but if you had stuck in the money in 1980 and left it for twenty years you'd have seen your money grow by roughly that amount every year.

Now let's look at the twenty-year period from 2000 to 2020. The oldest of the millennials would have come of age just before 2000 and the savvy ones among them may have started to invest some of their money as a way to beat inflation and hopefully get a better return on their cash. The figures for this time period are disappointing, with an average annual return of 6.76 per cent.

You might be thinking, 'Okay, but wasn't inflation super-duper high in the eighties?' I hear you! Adjusting the figures for inflation is important. You want to know how much your money would have grown in real terms. But even when we do this, it is the same dismal picture. The period from 1980 to 2000 works out at 12.21 per cent, with the following twenty years trailing at 4.71 per cent.[2]

Let's look at some hypothetical figures here, to make comparing those percentages a little bit easier. If say you had stuck £10,000 into the S&P 500 in 1980, by 2000 it would be worth approximately £200,000. Yet if you'd have stuck that £10,000 into the stock market in 2000, the resulting figure in 2020 would be closer to £37,000. Yup! You read those figures correctly. There's over £160,000 between the two final figures.

What does this mean then? Ultimately, it means that when millennials and Gen Z have taken their first tentative steps into the world of investing the results have been VERY disappointing. Our money has not had the ability to work nearly as hard for us as it did for the likes of the boomers and the Gen Xers. The stock market is giving us so much less and therefore we need to do more if we want to get even close to those dizzying returns of our predecessors.

Let's Chat about Pensions

There are many areas of finance where our generations have drawn the short straw. So, unfortunately, I can go on. Pensions.

Prior to the 1980s, defined benefit (DB) pensions were fairly standard. If you had a pension, chances are it was one of these. Basically, this is a scheme that would pay you an income for life based on your salary and years of service.

In the years, following this, the DB pension fell out of favour and a shift was made towards defined contribution pensions. These are where you pay into a pot and that pot is invested. I have already told you about what has been going on with investing recently, so you have probably already worked out that this would be problematic. Some might even say disastrous.

DB pensions still exist and are mostly found in public sector positions such as the NHS and teaching. They are considered some of the best pensions out there, but they aren't as good as they once were. In the last decade or two, many DB pensions have shifted from a final salary model to a career average, which many consider a worse deal.

The changes to pensions also come with changes to the retirement age and the age at which you can access your pension. Thanks to better healthcare, we are living longer. This means that our pensions need to last longer. There are now basically two options: work for longer or pay more in to cover those costs. Some people have to do both.

Cost of Living Increases

At the time of writing this book before its initial publication, there is additional grim financial news to contend with. Inflation is at a 40-year high and continuing to rise. This means that the cost of everything from food to clothes to rent is rising significantly and, to make it worse, wages are largely stagnant.

Paying for these everyday items, and the luxury ones too, is relatively more expensive. Mere survival has become more costly in real terms. The last time inflation was climbing as it is now was in the seventies and eighties, so you can shut down any boomer who tries to use that one against you. You are contending with the same financial misery they did and MORE. Remember the declining stock market returns, house price increases and worsening pension? So you have my full permission to ssshh anyone who suggests that youngsters today have it easy.

Alongside all this financial doom and gloom are the many world-altering events that we have had to live through and which have shaped and reshaped society. I am thinking about 9/11, when as kids we watched the horror unfold on TV and then saw the aviation industry change forever. Then there was the global recession of 2008–09, when jobs, banks and your favourite high street shops were disappearing in droves. Then, after a decade of attempting to recover from this, we are dealing with a pandemic, climate crisis and war in Eastern Europe.

Aside from the financial implications of these events, they have affected us in ways that we cannot see or quantify. While my childhood was pumped full of optimism for the future, reality hit hard when terrorism burst into life in my teenage years. The 7/7 bombings in London brought that closer to home and made me suspicious of unattended bags on all forms of public transportation. In my early adulthood, I wrestled with the reality that the career in finance that I had been toying with may not be possible, as banks around the world folded or were bailed out by governments.

And this has gone on and on. You might think that millennials have the potential to be one of the most resilient generations, after all that we have lived through. But this all takes a toll. Emotionally and financially!

Please Universe! Just Give Us a Break!

In fairness, the boomers lived through all this too. But they had a couple of moderately uneventful decades in their twenties and thirties, when they could get their heads down, save, invest, buy property; and then, when their kids started clearing off to uni and the world went a little wild, they sat in their mortgage-free homes, with their pensions growing nicely, and watched it all happen on the TV while ordering a takeaway.

We didn't have that luxury, so cut yourself some slack.

I hope by now you have realised that your latte, Netflix, easyJet and gym habits are not the problem. It is not you, it is actually harder for us than it was for our parents and grandparents. (At this point, despite all the above evidence, I am still fully expecting some boomer to accuse me of being a lazy, socialist snowflake in a review. Jeff, mate! Facts are facts – don't come at me!).

You are allowed at this point to have a little cry and a sulk. If there is one thing that we have more of than past generations, it is emotional awareness, and we are going to lean into that. Let it out!

Personally, I feel that knowing that the situations are not comparable makes me feel better. I no longer feel the need to look at where my parents were at my age and chastise myself for not being in the same place as them. The world is different now, so why on Earth would I be the same?

Furthermore, why would I want to be the same?

Why would YOU want to be the same?

Reasons to Be Cheerful?

Let's now look at the good stuff. The stuff that has changed gives us more freedoms and, if done correctly, a greater chance at being financially secure than those generations before us.

One of the biggest changes, which has undeniably had a huge impact, is the internet. Or just the rise of technology in our daily lives. Unlike our parents and grandparents, we have grown up in a digital world.

Millennials are considered to be the first digital natives. As a millennial myself, I grew up seeing the technological world unfold before my eyes. I remember my infant school getting its first ever computer and being given the role of 'figuring it out' by my teacher. What followed was weeks of tinkering and making computer-related excuses to get out of PE.

I saw my parents buy our first home computer (a lovely black and green screen with a printer that spooled paper from a roll), and the upgrades that followed eventually brought the internet to our lives, and with it the joys of MSN Messenger and Neopets.

Mobile phones became a normal part of life when I hit 13, and suddenly I was in constant connection with the world, even if it did cost me 10p a time and 'I had 2 ryt lyk dis'. But I quickly got upgrades, and eventually had access to the entire internet from the palm of my hand and with it the world.

Many would say that Gen Z and Gen Alpha are the true digital natives. Where millennials had to learn as they went along, the youngest generations have grown up in a world where digital is the default.

This presents us with opportunities that were out of reach and incomprehensible to older generations. Let's explore some examples.

Education, Education, Education

Firstly, education has never been more accessible. If you want to learn a new skill or refresh your current skills, you no longer have to go to evening classes. You can sign up to near enough any course online and work on your qualifications in your own time. This level of convenience allows you to find new ways to make money. You could even self-teach from YouTube and start a career in this way, essentially for free.

Between 2007 and 2019, the percentage of people who said that they had taken an online learning course grew from 4 per cent to 17 per cent,[3] and I'd be willing to bet that that figure rose substantially in 2020 and will likely continue to do so.

This means that good education is available wherever you live. You could live in the middle of nowhere and, as long as you have an internet connection, study for an MBA if you so desire. With the perks of never having to leave your home or get dressed. It also removes many barriers to learning previously experienced by sections of society, such as disabled people or parents with young children.

Speaking personally, this has served me well in recent years. As mentioned earlier, I struggle with my hearing. It is only a bit, but I always hated going to lectures as I could never hear what was being said. Even in 2006, it was rare that typed notes were available, and the sessions themselves were normally a human photocopying exercise where the professor would write their notes on the board and we would frantically scribble them down.

Now though, when I study online I always have the option of subtitles on video, a transcription or notes that I can print and read through. It has made learning that much more accessible to me and I am sure that I am not alone in being grateful for these advances.

There have been changes in the world of work too. With the Covid-19 pandemic, the opportunities for remote working grew exponentially. Roles and salaries that were formerly reserved for those living in or near major cities have opened up the world to everyone.

You can now work at your high-paying 'London-based' career from a cabin in the countryside. Or perhaps it means that you don't have to take a pay cut to stay close to where your parents live, or that you can raise your kids in the forest while chasing your career goals.

Better still, you can just grab your laptop and hop on a plane at your leisure. (Well, if your boss permits it.) More and more people are choosing careers that offer them the flexibility to work from around the world, and are blurring the lines between work and play.

In 2021, 31 per cent of businesses reported that the majority of their workforce was working remotely, and we are continuing with this trend.[4] What is most interesting is that 25–34-year-olds are the most likely to be working remotely, with 54 per cent of this age group doing so. Once again millennials and Gen Z are leading the way.

Now, this has a lot of financial benefits too which I will explore in more detail in the chapters ahead; but, as a little taster, it could mean that you can benefit from purchasing a home in the north of England while earning south-east England wages. The best of both worlds.

Since setting up my own business, I have been living this existence. My work is nearly entirely online, which is how I designed my business to be. I wanted to have the flexibility to live where I wanted, work where I wanted, but most of all to be there to pick up my kids from school every day. And I wanted to occasionally do stuff purely for fun in the middle of the day just because I could. I like to call that enjoying my life, and it works perfectly for me.

Changing the Way We Manage Our Money

The advancements in the digital landscape have not just impacted the way we work, but also how we manage and access our finances. Fintech is one of the UK's fastest-growing industries, and investment in the sector grew sevenfold between 2020 and 2021, from $5.2 billion to $37.3 billion.[5]

What on Earth is fintech though?

Fintech is the name given to technology that is improving the finance space. Some of this is happening behind the scenes within business, but much of it is happening in the consumer sphere, where you and I can see the direct benefits.

One of the key improvements in this area is in retail investing. This is basically investing that is done by normal people rather than companies. Your understanding of what investing looks like might come from films such as *The Wolf of Wall Street* where white men in suits shout at each other. BUY BUY BUY! SELL SELL SELL! Plus, lots of confusing-looking tables and graphs. But thanks to developments in this field, investing for normal people is now much calmer. You don't need to be all shouty to invest.

There now exist apps that enable you to invest in a range of companies or bonds (don't worry, all jargon will be covered in Chapter Ten) with a few simple clicks. Or if you aren't sure what to invest in, a robo-adviser can take a couple of details about your financial goals, income and risk level and suggest a fund that could best suit you. You can then either make a one-off payment or set up a regular amount. You can be as involved or as hands-off as you want to be.

Previous generations did not have this luxury. Investing used to be reserved for the wealthy or those who had the time and motivation to learn to do it. Most people would go to a financial adviser and pay high fees to have someone else invest their money on their behalf. Many in this situation would have to trust that the person they were handing their money to had their best interests at heart.

Thanks to fintech, it has never been easier both to learn

about investing and to actually invest. The same is true of pensions. You can look your pension statement up online whenever you like rather than waiting for it to come through the post. Plus, if you have 'lost' an old pension there are systems now that will find them for you. Literally, you can enter a few details into one of these apps and they will set their team to work to hunt down pensions in your name.

There are similar advancements happening all over the personal finance space. You can access your bank accounts through your phone and send money to your mates around the world. You can see automatically generated graphs that tell you where you have been spending all your money. You can buy house insurance that acknowledges that you are using smart tech to keep your house safe, and lower your premiums. You can do something similar with your car insurance too. There are even apps out there that will tell you the best ways to pay off your debt.

This is all fabulous and there is no doubt that this level of innovation will accelerate in the years to come. But the question is, where are you supposed to learn about all this?

What Does All This Mean for You?

The fast-changing nature of the personal finance space, combined with the diminishing returns from the old ways of managing money, means that you have to both unlearn the old ways and learn new ways of doing things. You live in a world of conflicting messaging, and figuring out what you need to pay attention to and what you don't is bloody exhausting.

On top of this, you probably have a house that needs cleaning, a social life that needs maintenance, a family that wants your attention, perhaps a partner who is seeking your affections, and you are supposed to feed yourself and stay at least mildly presentable. Then you are meant to have your shit together when it comes to your money too.

I'll say it again: CUT YOURSELF SOME SLACK!

Don't put so much pressure on yourself to be perfect. To be hitting the milestones. To know about everything that is going on in the finance world. Things have changed a lot, some good and some bad, and you are totally forgiven for not knowing how you 'should' be doing things.

On that note, I should say that there is no one right way to do things. I fear sounding rather clichéd here, but personal finance is personal. You have to find your own path with it.

Just as this book is breaking away from the financial rites of former generations, you too may need to break away from the rules that your friends, family and social circles would have you believe are the norm.

You will learn about multiple different areas of money management as you turn the pages of this book, but do not think that I am telling you exactly what you should be doing. Instead, I am daring you to find the perfect solution for you. This could look like a slight twist on what your parents taught you, or you may choose something even more radical than what you read ahead.

Therefore, I would urge you to take your journey to financial freedom slowly.

This is not a copy-and-paste job where you can take what your mum, dad, brother, sister, friend or colleague is doing and apply that to your life. This is more like learning to code. You need to know the building blocks to create a system that works for you. Truly personalised. You wouldn't expect to create the perfect code on the first attempt after reading a book about it. Instead, you'd try something and reflect. Then try again, making modifications and trying new things for size as you went along. Until one day you have something that makes sense for you.

It also helps to know a bit more than just what works for you in your current situation, as that could change over time. For example, you might not be looking for long-term housing solutions at this point, but there might come a time when you want to find somewhere more permanent to live. It would be handy for you to know the best approach for this. Don't worry; Chapter Six will give you some food for thought on that front.

Another area it's invaluable to have good knowledge about is how to handle debt. You might not currently be in debt but, if you experience a handful of unfortunate financial situations, you could be in need of tricks and tips to pay off a debt quickly. Being open to learning outside of what you immediately need is key. It gives you room to grow, adapt, and be prepared for whatever comes next.

Long before I decided to commit my life to teaching financial education online, I realised that I needed to learn how to invest. It was not something my parents taught me (they aren't investors) and I certainly wasn't taught about it in school. And at the time, I didn't have the money to invest. I was on maternity leave with my eldest and making every pay cheque count.

In the past, though, I had heard friends talk about how they had made money by investing, and I was fascinated; but I had literally no idea where to start. Even if I had had a few quid spare at that point I couldn't have invested it in anything, because I had no idea how to get my money into the stock market. The best I could do with my knowledge at the time was to either buy premium bonds or get some sort of fixed-term savings account with a slightly higher interest rate. But I wanted to know how to get my hands on a slice of the big names out there, like Apple, Amazon and Facebook. They were making loads of money and I wanted some of that.

This was a slow journey. I mean, I was a new mum, but more importantly I wanted to get it right. I read books about it, watched YouTube videos, read blog posts and scrolled through hundreds of reviews for different platforms. Remember, all of this was long before I needed to use the knowledge or really had that much to invest. Eventually, I felt like I was ready to take the plunge and start investing. I invested £2 that day. It may seem like a pointless amount, but it was the first step.

Now, I am a confident investor. I know the strategy that works for me. What is even better is that I know how to change my strategy to suit my circumstances. I have taken the time to learn the style of investing that will work for me for years. It feels good to have developed those skills. And it felt good to know before I needed to know; to have taken it at a leisurely pace and enjoyed the journey, while ensuring that I knew all the different options, outcomes and risks involved.

The point is that, in this rapidly changing world of money, it is okay to feel like you don't understand or that the opportunities available to previous generations no longer exist. You don't need to hit arbitrary milestones like getting on the property ladder before you are 30 or having investments of twice your annual salary, but you need to know what you do want and take some steps to get there.

You have my permission to let go of lofty expectations and to slow things down. You can't do it all and know it all. However, you must do and know some things and be taking action towards that, like I did even when I didn't have a penny to invest. What those things are will be entirely down to you. There's a lot in this book that will help you with that process.

Remember – cut yourself some slack. You are not your parents, your friends, your grandparents, or those people on social media. You are you and you are living in a time that has never existed before. If you take a bit of time to figure out how to thrive in your own unique way then I would say that is time well spent.

In the following chapters, the focus is going to move away from what happened in the past and instead be on the future. You will learn a host of new strategies to apply to all areas of your personal finances.

It is quite possible that you will strongly disagree with some of what I say. That is to be expected. Society has been telling you one way of managing your money for so long that anything else is going to feel like a threat to your understanding. You might also feel overwhelmed – like you have SO MUCH to do and there is not enough time to do it. Again, this is normal. Many people who I have worked with over the years feel like they need to sort out their savings, pay off their debt and start investing immediately. You don't. You do need to slow yourself down and reflect.

And remember, it is not you – it is the system. You have spent years trying to fit a square peg (your financial freedom) into a round hole (current financial system). It'll take time to reshape that peg. It doesn't mean that you shouldn't do it, though. Reading and learning from this book is a great initial step towards a financial future that suits you and is achievable in this day and age.

Chapter Two

Freeing Yourself from Expectations

In a world full of influencers, it is hard to know if you have ever had a true longing for anything real. Sometimes it can feel like all the things you want are just someone else's dream. Or even plain old marketing.

You are not alone if you feel like this. Heck! I have a list on my phone of stuff that I want and most of it is because someone has it already and now I want it too. It ranges from stuff I have seen my mates wearing to random nonsense that popped up on TikTok and I felt my life was incomplete without.

But how do you work out what you really want? And what does it mean for your finances?

Over the course of my life, I have had periods of spending and periods of saving. Rarely have these two overlapped successfully. Naturally, even in the saving periods there was still necessary expenditure happening, and vice versa. But if I took a zoomed-out view of my life, I would be able to go, 'Oh yeah – that's when I was saving to go travelling' or 'that's when I spent all that money on travelling.' Or 'We were saving to buy a house then' followed by 'Look at us – buying a house and filling it with furniture and memories.'

The fact is that whenever I have had a spendy phase it has been massively helped by having a saving phase beforehand. Literally, the former has rarely been possible without the latter. But also the reverse is true.

Without the motivation of some fantastic reason to have money to spend, it is really hard to save. I know! I have tried MANY times in my life to save money without a goal and it has never worked out well. Yeah, I've saved a bit, but never anything that is going to change the world. But cor blimey, when I have had a good goal to focus on the savings have piled up in no time at all.

What's the Evidence Though?

Good question! Research by NS&I (National Savings & Investments) found that people who set a savings goal not only saved faster but also saved £550 more per year than those who did not.[6] And if that extra cash in your bank account isn't motivational enough, then think of all the other benefits.

When you have a goal you can make smaller goals! What? Yep! No one aims to save an entire retirement pot. Well, they might but you'll want to do some celebrating along the way. You might celebrate the first £1,000 you've got in your pension pot, then £10k, then £20k, and so on and so forth until you hit retirement and go on a cruise.

Oh and, if you aren't the sort of person that celebrates the small victories, then why not? Everyone loves praise and self-praise is the best! There's nothing like feeling super smug because you achieved something that you didn't even tell your mum about. Honestly, silent smugness feels great!

Psychology professor Dr Gail Matthews at Michigan State University conducted a study into the importance of goal setting. She discovered that 76 per cent of those people who wrote down their goals, made a plan to achieve them and got their friends to help smashed them.[7]

By comparison, of the people who didn't do these things only 43 per cent made their goals a reality, so that's a pretty big difference. I don't know about you but I find that 33 per cent gap in success rate pretty motivating.

Another study found that setting goals was linked with higher motivation, self-esteem, self-confidence and autonomy.[8] These are all massively desirable qualities that you are probably working hard to cultivate in your life, and it all comes from having goals.

Let's take this another step further. One study by Yukl and Latham[9] (coincidentally they are both called Gary, and that makes me giggle for some reason) found that, when people were set goals either by themselves or by other people, those with more challenging goals achieved greater success.

This blows my mind.

But it does make sense when you look at it sensibly. Let's say you set a goal to save £100 over a couple of months. You start sticking money in your bank account and you get 90 per cent of the way there (£90, for those of you who are mathematically challenged) and think, 'Ah that's good enough!'

What if you had set a higher goal? Let's say you pushed yourself to save £200 instead. You work on it and get to the £90 mark again. You ain't gonna stop there, are you? You didn't even make it halfway to your goal. So you keep going. You go past that £100 mark and you might make it to £150, or even much closer to £200. By setting a goal that stretches you, you are more likely to achieve more than if you set something lower. Even if you don't reach that goal.

And evidence aside, how often do you hear about people who were just randomly saving and one day they realised, 'Oh bloody hell! I have enough to buy a house!' Practically never, right?

Savings goals are the driving force that gets you where you want in life. You decide on what you wanna do and then you go ahead and get busy to make it happen. You write them down, work out how much you need to make them happen, you set up that bank account and watch it all work out.

Easy peasy, right?

Well, not exactly! This chapter is all about looking past the marketing, the influencers, the TikTok shop nonsense, and deciding what you actually want to save for. And this is connected to those very big questions.

What Do You REALLY Want from Life?

That's the question that plagues most of us. At the root of most of our worries and stresses, whether you are dealing with money concerns or health issues, or debating your career path, is likely 'Is this how I want my life to be?' Trying to figure it all out is overwhelming. Most people sort of give up trying to work it out and just focus on getting through the day in front of them. And that's great and all. But what if you want more?

Here's an exercise for you. Grab a notebook and a pen and find a quiet spot to sit and just exist for a bit. Then I want you to imagine you've opened your eyes after the most perfect sleep. But you aren't waking up to any old situation. You are waking up to your dream life.

What does that look like?

This is your ideal day. You've opened your eyes and where are you? What does your bedroom look like? What can you see, feel, smell and hear? Who is lying next to you? What can you see from the window?

You need to be writing all this down. It helps if you can get really clear on the details too. Think about what your bedding looks like, the colours, and the fabrics. Then think about the temperature. Is it warm or cool?

You know that film *Groundhog Day*, where Bill Murray gets stuck doing the same day over and over? You need to be writing down the details of that day that you would be HAPPY to live over and over again. Unlike poor Bill, I want you to decide what that perfect day would look like and then set about making it your day-to-day reality.

After you've dealt with waking up, you go through the rest of your day. Are you having breakfast in bed? Or are you having breakfast at the table with your partner and a gorgeous horde of children? Maybe you are working out first? Or jumping straight in the shower?

What about work? Do you work from home (WFH)? Or in an office? Or maybe you work in the forest with the most amazing team of researchers? I dunno what floats your boat, so that's for you to decide.

Once you are done with this exercise, you will have a much clearer idea of what you want from your life. From the materialistic stuff to the people you want to spend your life with to the emotions that you want to feel on a day-to-day basis.

It is quite a chunky task, so you might want to step away from it for a couple of days and let it sit. Then read through it again later. Add in any tweaks that you have reflected on that you feel would be important to you. Whenever I do this activity, there are always bits that I think of afterwards that I'm like, 'Oh yeah! I want one of those!' (normally stuff like regular massages or a butler to run my baths.)

It doesn't matter what you put on this list really. It just has to be what YOU want. Don't do this exercise with other people, as you'll get swayed by their influences. I want you to get to know yourself a little better. And most importantly, work out what you want to aim towards. This vision for your life is now your ultimate goal.

A good next step is now to break this goal down into smaller goals. So it could be that you had a vision of your dream house. That's one. Then maybe you wanted a family.

That's two. Then maybe you are in cracking physical and mental health. That's three. And then maybe you have this awesome career. That's four. Etc.

Obviously, your life doesn't have to be like that at all. It could be that your goals are more like waking up in a different part of the world every week. Goal 1. Running your own business. Goal 2. A massive investment portfolio that subsidises your lifestyle. Goal 3. Or any combination of the above and more, as long as it makes you tick.

What you are aiming for is to have something to work towards. That lifestyle you described in the activity is linked to the feelings you are seeking. I imagine there are emotions tied up with that dream home, the business you want to build and the family you hope to create. You need to turn it into the practical and the obtainable. Stuff that you can start working towards, saving for and putting into motion. Thankfully, you can lean into these emotions for motivation. Imagine the feeling of stepping into that dream home and then use that as your driving force to open that savings account. Or the sense of freedom that will come from running your own business to get the website up and running.

Looking at these lists of goals though probably has you wanting to run to your bed, pull the duvet over your head and have a little cry at the seeming impossibility of the whole thing. Big goals are intimidating, BUT remember: the more challenging the goal, the more likely we are to be successful. So try not to panic and instead think about all the amazing stuff you are going to make happen along the way.

I will at this point in the book allow you to take a break. By getting this far and acknowledging that you have these big goals, you have already done more work in sorting out your finances than most people you know. You've got goals and they are super-duper powerful. Even if all you do is write them down every day, you'll be more likely to make them happen than those who don't.

But you can do better than that.

Remember that research by Dr Gail Matthews? Well, as part of it she said that you have to make an action plan. What that means is putting some steps into place to get to those goals. Some milestones. A ladder of smaller steps that takes you to these lofty heights.

Your next step is to pick one of those goals. Like buying your dream house. Then figure out some medium-sized steps to getting there. The following chapters will talk more about the different areas of your finances and how to maximise these opportunities, so don't worry if this makes you sweat a little bit.

The smaller the steps you can put in place the better. It makes the whole thing far less daunting and much more achievable. Getting your first £1,000 in the bank for your first home seems waaaayyy more doable than buying a million-pound beach house.

You will still be on that journey to that big goal, but taking smaller steps and focusing on the small stuff will help you stay much more motivated.

Let me give you an example of what these smaller steps might look like:

ULTIMATE GOAL: FREEDOM TO PLAN YOUR DAY AS YOU PLEASE

1. Learn some skills – get some qualifications in a field that will make you some money.
2. Get a job in that profession – build up some experience and get your name out there a bit.
3. Start a side hustle – use these skills to start making extra money on the side.
4. Build a strong emergency fund – get a pot of money together that you can fall back on when you go self-employed.
5. Go self-employed – pull the plug and go fully in on working for yourself and planning your days as you please.
6. Take it further – build systems and employ people to make money for you.
7. Enjoy all that extra freedom.

Honestly? These are more medium-sized steps. I'm not immune to seeing 'learn some skills' and rolling my eyes. This stuff takes time, and you would be bang on the money if you were thinking that maybe you need to break these steps down further.

So let's take each point one at a time and slice them up into smaller goals.

When you do this, 'learn some skills' becomes:

1. Research suitable courses – compile a list of courses

that will give you the skills and qualifications you need to reach your goals.
2. Save up – set a goal to save the money for the course.
3. Sign up – get your name on that course list.
4. Complete assignment 1.
5. Complete assignment 2 etc etc blah blah – you get it!
6. Submit the final assignment – get all that paperwork in and feel a wave of relief.
7. Celebrate your new skills – allow yourself to enjoy achieving this goal.

The point here is not that achieving any of this is easy. It is that you can make it more manageable, and subsequently more achievable, by creating a plan of action. And then by doing it. Obvs!

How to Know What You DON'T Want

You have now spent a fair bit of time thinking and reflecting on what you want. But what about what you don't want? Logically, it seems that knowing what you don't want might be the most natural thing in the world. Realistically, it can be bloody hard!

As children, our world is shaped by those around us. You learn how the world works by seeing the adults in your life respond to the stuff that goes on around them. Your parents will shape your initial views. From them, you will learn what is exciting, what is disappointing, what is socially acceptable, what is the correct way to act, and so on and so forth.

I see this a lot in the classroom. The students sitting in front of me will share an opinion that I know is straight from the mouths of their parents. Nothing wrong with that, but when you see it happening to other people it makes you question your own conditioning too.

This is what happened to me. As I said in the introduction, I had a cracking childhood. My parents adored me, loving home, great house, own bedroom, regular holidays and all the after-school clubs. It is not surprising that I looked at my parents and thought they had life sussed.

You might have gone through the same thing – or perhaps you experienced the opposite. Maybe growing up was crappy for you. The grown-ups in your life struggled and life felt tough. This may have led you to want something different for you.

Family are not our only influence, though, so let's take a look at what happens outside of family life.

You probably had some friends too, and they came with their own rights, wrongs and thoughts on how to do this thing called life. Some of these will have rubbed off on you as you tried to fit in and feel accepted. You might also have been like, 'Yeah actually, that looks like a better way of doing things than I am used to' and wanted to incorporate these new things into your personality.

To clarify, I'm talking about everything from the way you conduct yourself in public to the more consumerist elements like what clothes look good and what music you should listen to.

Over the years, as we meet more people, we add and remove different elements. Your opinions change as the world around you changes, whether those changes be your partner, your friends, your workplace, where you live or your exposure to media. What you wanted from your life ten years ago could be very different from what you want now, and that's okay.

Therefore, it is important to spend some time working on what YOU want. In this moment. Right now. It is what matters to you in the present, and how you are going to focus on that, that is important.

Try to shake off the old versions of you that come with their own wants and desires. Even more importantly, ditch other people's wants for you, whether this is what your parents think you should do, or silent, unseen nudges from social media feeds, or disapproving looks from friends and distant relatives.

When you sift out the 'don't wants', what you are left with is your ideal life. Or a vision for it. How did this match up with what you thought you wanted?

Whichever path you take to figure out what you want, the key is to get clear and laser-focused on achieving it. Leave behind the parts of your life that don't light you up, wave goodbye to the expectations of other people, and clear your path for a version of your life that brings you joy.

Chapter Three

Getting Paid

This might be my favourite, and the most important, chapter in the whole book. Because, firstly, who doesn't love making money? And because, secondly, how we make money and how much of it can dictate our whole existence and experience of this thing called life.

Our job takes up multiple hours out of every week and elements like the people we meet there, the conditions that we work in and the quality of our commute are going to have a sizeable impact on our day-to-day life. It can be the difference between a life we love and a life we loathe.

Unfortunately, for most of us there's no escaping this. We have to make money, and working is the main way that we make that happen.

Thankfully, we still have some choices left about HOW we make it happen.

Charlotte Jessop

What to Do When You Grow Up

Sometimes I look back and feel like I had limited options when it came to my career. As a child, I was blessed with a mathematical brain, and not only that but I bloody loved it too. Despite being bullied regularly for this by my sister (who will still imitate me by sliding her glasses back up her nose and saying, 'According to my calculations'), I powered on and studied maths at university. I had thought about niching down and doing something like accounting or civil engineering, but decided to keep my options open instead.

In true millennial style, a global disaster came along and set things back for me, in the form of the 2008–09 credit crunch. So there was little old me with a mathematics degree in a world where banks were slashing their graduate programmes because they were receiving bailouts from the government. Suddenly there were far fewer careers out there.

But the world was desperate for mathematics teachers and they were offering a few grand as a golden hello for anyone who fancied giving it a go. So that's what I did. I trained as a teacher.

Now, I don't regret that choice. I have made good money as a maths teacher, and discovered that I was a pretty good one at that. Oh, and I LOVED that the world was desperate for maths teachers. I love feeling needed!

But do I feel like I was an active participant in choosing my career? Well, no not really!

After being told that a maths degree would open so

many doors for me by every school careers adviser and her cat, when I reached twenty-one there were a lot of shut doors. I wasn't alone in this experience either. Many people of my age found themselves in careers that fell short of where they wanted to be, or on a career path that was nothing like what they had envisioned for themselves.

The moral of this story though is: that is okay.

Long gone is the era of train in a field, get a job, work for your employer for 40 years, and then retire with a nice gold watch and a lifetime of service. Our generation is shaking things up and I genuinely believe that we are much better for it.

I worked as a maths teacher for ten years. I had a few promotions in that time too, studied for some extra qualifications that would make me better at what I did, and for a long time thrived. Until one day it wasn't what I wanted any more. I had a couple of kids by this point and my life view had shifted. I didn't want to be flogging my kipper for a job that left me so tired at the end of the day that I didn't want to play with my kids or go out and see my friends or participate in my hobbies. I wanted to be more present in the world that I had created for myself.

Every day I count my blessings that I am alive when I am, because the internet is a wonderful thing. It has changed the way we work and connect with the world. If I had been a part of my mum's generation, I just know I would have been one of those women having Tupperware parties; I'm entrepreneurial and, without the worldwide web, I would have definitely resorted to flogging my mates crap they didn't want.

Luckily, I've had access to the internet since I was a teenager, and I decided at some point during my thirtieth year on this planet that I was going to forge a new path for myself, and started writing about personal finance online. The short version of this story is that several years later you ended up reading this book.

Deciding what you want to do to make money is no longer a 'one-and-done' decision. Now we change things up and follow our heads, our hearts, our friends and the money into any job that we think will be a good fit. We pick up skills from one job and think, 'You know what, I'm bloody good at that – I think I'll see if someone else will pay me more to do that elsewhere.'

Studying is no longer a one-time deal either. No one leaves school or uni and uses those skills and only those skills for the rest of their life. Hell, I know people who have done three degrees in pursuit of their perfect career. But equally, there are people who do shorter courses to get skills that just give them a little leg-up in the world. Or they study just because something sparks their interest. I'll tell you this – studying because it lights up your heart in some way is THE BEST reason to study.

As a result of this significantly less linear approach to working and careers, the world is now full of people who are making money in fantastically unique and exciting ways. It is just what the world needs. Creative solutions to the modern world.

Emma Gannon has a marvellous book called *The Multi-*

Hyphen Method that beautifully describes what I am talking about here. She describes a 21st-century workforce as being made up of people who are doing lots of different things all at once. You might be a Writer-Marketer-Content Creator or a Photographer-Florist-Engineer or an Accountant-Scuba Diver Instructor.

The message here is that you have more options than ever before, and you don't have to pick one and spend the rest of eternity slogging away at it in exchange for a watch you'll never wear. You can pick and change and choose to do something different at any point. Your career will be filled with hundreds of choices about where to work, how to do it, and what you could do next. Making money has never been more fun. But it does require us to be a bit more ballsy in the process; take more risks and chase after something a little better. It requires us to keep learning and taking an interest in the world.

Learning as You Go

A big part of what inspired me to study maths at uni was the money. (What can I say? I love money!). I knew the careers that would be available to me as a maths graduate could pay well, and I wanted me a slice of that.

Earning potential is a huge factor in our decisions about what we do for work. There is a subtle subconscious nudging of societal pressures that is forever pushing us in the direction of the job that is going to pay us the most money. And we want that for ourselves. Who doesn't want a life of comfort and luxury over one of struggle and hardship?

The question then is how you find the career that earns you the most money.

Well, you can't. There's no real way of knowing which career path is going to give you the best financial prospects. You just do your best at any one time and hope that works out for you.

One key component is education. The better your education the greater the options that are open to you. Unfortunately, that doesn't end at school. You can't do a few GCSEs and hope for the best. I believe that education is lifelong, and it is probably this mentality that has led me to become a multi-hyphenate myself. Ongoing education, both formal and informal, allows you to increase your value. This may be within your sector, or perhaps you have had to go self-employed and realise your value yourself. More on that in a bit.

With education, you can forge your own career path, learn what you are good at, and bring more and more skills and wisdom to what you do. This constant growth means that whatever job you find yourself in you can make it work for you.

Conventionally, qualifications and training are the ideal way to build your skill set and increase your desirability in the workforce marketplace. Plus this style of education normally leads to formally recognised certification, which makes it easier to convince others that you have the talent that they are looking for.

With the world of online education growing at a rapid

pace, it has never been easier to study from home around your work, family and other commitments. The launch of Open University in 1969 changed the way that we learn and ensured that education could be accessed regardless of location. Then government grants and, ultimately, the Student Loans Company helped many wannabe students overcome financial barriers to education. As a result, the current workforce is the best educated in history.

But education is more than degrees and qualifications. Learning is a passion, a hobby and a joy. I bloody love learning. The sense of empowerment that I get from knowing something new or getting to question my viewpoints or opinions Lights. Me. Up. Therefore, the idea that I am going to restrict that to whatever course I am signed up for at that time is bonkers to me. Instead, I seek out new learning opportunities constantly, in much more informal ways. Once again, the rise of the internet and 'content culture' is key here; it means that we are constantly connected to an endless stream of knowledge. Whatever we want to know is at our fingertips and we can use this to upskill ourselves any time or place.

When I first started my business I was clueless about how to create a website, but I knew I needed one. It was a blog, after all. I wasn't getting far in that world without one. But I didn't have the funds to pay someone else to build it for me. So I watched a gazillion YouTube videos and read a quintillion blog posts on the subject until I had something that I felt I could put out into the world.

Now I am never going to make building websites my career, but over the last six years I have been able to help many of my friends and family to build their websites. Furthermore, I have been able to build, make money from, and eventually sell many of my own. If I think about how much money I have made, both directly and indirectly, from a skill that I learned from the internet in my PJs, it is easily in multiple six figures. And I wouldn't even list this as a skill on my CV. It is just something I learned out of necessity.

You probably have a whole host of things like this that you know loads about but that you wouldn't even consider yourself an expert in. Others on my list would include paddleboarding, gluten-free diets, breastfeeding, organisation, travelling with two small kids, and I'm not too bad at self-PR either. Am I putting any of these things on my CV? Hell no! Well, I stick the paddleboarding and the travel stuff under the interests section to make myself look a little more well-rounded, but that's about it.

Did I go to university to learn about any of these? Nope! Do I have a certificate in these skills? Again, nope! Did I just spend years being passionate about each of them and reading endless books, articles and blog posts or watch all the videos about them? Damn right that's what happened.

It is highly unlikely that I will ever seek to make money from any of these random skills. Rather, they give me the power to know that I can become an expert in whatever the hell I fancy if I become sufficiently interested in it. And all of these skills can feed into who I am as a person and what I can bring to my career and my job at the time. It is an amazing world that we are living in!

What about Self-Employment Then?

In my opinion, self-employment is the pinnacle of getting paid. You get to choose what you do, when you do it, where you do it and who you do it with. There are no other forms of work that give you that privilege and I think it is something that is so untapped in terms of bringing more money, and happiness, into our lives.

However, I am not so far up my own rear orifice to realise that it may not be the dream for everybody. I know that for you this might be your idea of hell. And I get it. Employed work has its benefits and, for some people, it just works. Gosh, the financial stability, the structured hours and the consistency of the work are certainly appealing. There are plenty of people out there who have been employees their whole lives, made a truckload of money and wouldn't have wanted things any other way. Even in my life, I have had times when having a job has been just what I needed. It has given me peace of mind and the funds to achieve some other goals. It's totally okay to not think that self-employment is the pinnacle if you don't want to.

BUT I do think it is awesome!

On the day I wrote this chapter, I went for coffee with a former colleague. She had contacted me on LinkedIn and asked if I wanted to meet up and chat over what I had been doing since we stopped working together four to five years ago. Now this friend of mine had had a long and fantastic career as a teacher, assistant headteacher, and then deputy headteacher. But fourteen days previously, she had left the profession to pursue her own business ideas.

Now I love people like this. I can properly get behind a story of someone waking up and realising that they have had enough of life how it was before and are ready to grab the bull by the horns and do something about it. So I sipped my coffee, eyes wide, and sat riveted as she told me what she intended to do now.

Her story goes like this:

Eighteen months ago she started a motor racing team with her husband. Super cool, I know! It had been a passion of hers from a young age and it was something that she always wanted to do, so they decided to do it together. But she told me that this wasn't a project that she was doing to make money really. She has another idea for that. Alongside, the motor racing thing, she started a company that looks to support businesses in developing high-performance teams through well-being services.

Don't you just love that? This remarkable woman has left behind a financially secure and highly successful career because she wants to chase an alternative dream. As we walked back to the car after the coffee sesh, she said to me, 'I had a business lunch the other day. It was a big part of what I wanted for my life. In teaching, I would eat my lunch out of a plastic container, wearing a hi-vis, standing in the middle of a field. I think I deserve more than that from my life.'

And right there, in that simple goal, is the power of self-employment. You get to decide what you want your life to look like. You get to decide how long your lunch break is and where you to take it. You get to decide if you work with that client who sent you a snotty email or whether you tell them to take their contract and shove it.

The other lesson in my friend's story is that you can do a whole mix of stuff and still make money. She is the ultimate multi-hyphenate. By taking all the components of her life that she gets the most joy from, she is forging a career that allows her to do them all and still make money – and she is probably going to make a lot of it too. I totally believe in her.

Taking that leap into self-employment can be daunting. While being responsible for making your own money can feel like a liberation, it can also be a little terrifying. Or a lot terrifying if you've got a mortgage and a couple of kids, or an elderly parent to provide for. But it really doesn't have to be an all-or-nothing experience.

You know all those skills that you have been gleaning from YouTube or from those books that you read before bed every night? Well, you could find a way to turn that into a self-employed side hustle. Look at me: I took a love of money and all things finances and turned that from a side hustle into a full-time business.

While we are on side hustles, they have kind of gotten a bit of a bad rep. The concept of hustle culture and the rising need of families to work more than one job has forced some people to NEED a side hustle. I agree that there is a sadness in that. I don't think that anyone who works a full-time job should ever NEED to then go out and do a second job to make ends meet. I want side hustles to be a creative avenue that gives people the opportunity to test the waters of a new project, or practise new or old skills in a way that makes them feel inspired.

Self-employment via a side hustle is a great way to practise at what you ultimately want from the world of work. It supplies a platform for you to learn what you love and also what you hate. A space to really fine-tune your thoughts about how you want to make money and how you want to get paid. On top of that, a side hustle gives you another income source, which can contribute to your financial stability. Let's talk more about that.

What We THINK Financial Stability Looks Like, and What It Could Actually Be

If you ask my mum what financial stability is, she will probably say something along the lines of 'having a good job that pays the bills and gives you a little bit left over'. She might talk about having some money in the bank to cover the emergencies too. And yeah, she's probably bang on the money with that. If you'll pardon the pun!

But in this post-Covid world, where the cost of living crisis is breeding financial uncertainty, is this kind of financial stability achievable or sustainable?

Call me an optimist but I like to think this is something that we can all reach. It might just need a different approach. Yes, we are seeing rising costs when it comes to food, electricity, or literally anything else for that matter. But as we saw earlier, we also live in a world where our capacity to make and earn money has more potential than ever.

Now before you come at me all like, 'Yeah but Charlotte, not everyone can earn more money!' – I get it! I do! Making more money isn't necessarily easy; but I do believe that it is possible for everyone. Yes, EVERYONE! Hear me out, okay?

I used to be a teacher. As a public servant, I was destined for a career with government-determined pay scales and ultimately a life of very little control over what I earned. For the first six years of my teaching career, I would move up a pay point each year. Then that maxed out. After that, I had to convince my bosses that I was worthy of being allowed on to the next level of pay. But other than meeting the minimum requirements for this, there was little room to accelerate that pay increase or be awarded more for greater performance than another colleague.

Back then, I would have argued with anyone who said that making more money was possible. However, I decided to take a little look outside of the box and see if there were other avenues to contribute to increasing my income and ultimately improving my financial stability.

Turns out that I had a few options.

One of the easiest ways that I did this was by making sure I was getting the best interest rates on my savings. Without having to work any harder or begging my boss for a pay rise, I started to make more money.

Then I ventured into other ways that I could make

more money. I started by leveraging my teaching skills, and did some tutoring. I was practising the skills that I used every day and was able to use the extra income to bring more fun into my life. This was also my first step into the world of side hustling.

Eventually I started my personal finance business, which was a second income alongside my teaching job at the time. The realisation that I had the capacity to make money from more than just my day job was a huge relief. Apart from the benefits of having more money in my life, there was a sense of peace in knowing that, even if the teaching career went down the drain, I had another way to make money. That is a kind of financial stability.

Whereas for previous generations steady employment over many years was the answer to financial stability, now it is about having multiple income sources. All that we have discussed in this chapter contributes to this.

Gaining all those extra skills means that you have plenty of options for making money. Starting a side hustle gives you more money for your household finances. And later on in this book, I talk more about getting the most from your savings and investments, like I did by seeking out the best interest rates on my savings, so that you can earn an income from these too.

If the worst should happen and you lost your job, wouldn't it feel delightful to know that you had money coming in from elsewhere? Even if this wasn't to the same level as your job, it could be the difference between financial ruin and a period of financial hardship.

Back in 2020, my family and I had crash-landed in

the UK after travelling the world, because Covid was closing in around us. It had been my full intention to go back to teaching, but in March 2020 schools closed and no one knew when they would open again. What I once believed to be a career that would never see me without a job had left me in one of the trickiest situations of my life.

Desperate for a way to pay the bills and make sure that our kids didn't go without, I turned to my business. At that point, *Looking After Your Pennies* was barely more than a side hustle that was trickling money into my bank account. But it WAS making me money. I would make a few quid from recommending some products or services that had saved me money, and occasionally a company would pay me to promote them on my social media channels. I jumped in head first and expanded it in every way I could. I pitched to companies rather than waiting for them to come to me. I shared more of the things that I loved and told people where to buy them. The money shot up. My business saved our financial arses at that point, and it continues to show me the power of multiple income streams.

I don't think I will ever go back to depending on one stream of income. The more legs my stool has the more stable it will be, and this goes for my financial situation too. Do not restrict yourself to earning money in one way. Make sure that you have money trickling in from all over the place and you will find that your sense of financial security rises.

This chapter started by saying that how and how much

you get paid can have a significant impact on your happiness in life. And this is true. But in today's society that happiness can also come from how many different ways you get paid. Do what you love and the money will follow, as they say. You might have to do more than just one of the things that you love to achieve this; but, in my opinion, there is little wrong with that.

Chapter Four

What Is All This Tax?

Before you go ahead and skip this chapter because it sounds as dull as dishwater, I am going to urge you to stop right there. Tax education is super important. With the main benefit being that when you are tax-educated you can learn how to pay less of it and that is just wonderful.

A quick Google of 'what do we wish we had learned in school' gave me over a billion results and, out of the dozen or so that I bothered opening, money and tax appeared in all of them. Given that paying tax is basically unavoidable, why do so few of us actually understand it? Or more to the point, why don't we get taught about it?

You can probably guess that I am a huge advocate for financial education in schools. But, even if we fixed that problem today, it is not going to help you or the millions of other people who went through education in a time when money management was considered not important enough for a place in the curriculum.

Thank goodness then that you found this book. Because

I bridge the gap in your tax knowledge that your school was too busy to fill. (Oh, a quick note on this: I don't hold it against schools AT ALL. Having been a part of that system, I know that what schools are expected to do is huge and, until the government decides to prioritise financial education, fund the training of finance teachers and provide the money for resources and equipment to ensure the correct teaching of this topic, schools will always be on the back foot when it comes to being able to provide this.)

But you need to know, so let's get started on what tax is and why we pay it.

Taxation is used by the government to raise money for public sector spending. What this means is that by paying taxes you are contributing towards the costs of the things that we all get to enjoy as a collective. In the UK, this means your tax will go toward supporting schools, the NHS, the police force, the fire service, and at a more local level less obvious services such as street lighting, road maintenance and bin collections.

Interestingly, when surveyed back in 2021, over half of the British population (52 per cent) said that they would support an increase in taxes and ultimately public spending.[10] A further 40 per cent said that they would be happy to keep taxes as they were. Generally, despite the whinging and the sense of deflation when we look at our payslips, we support the idea of paying taxes and appreciate the benefits and services that they provide us.

Even though you may feel resentful at seeing a chunk

of your money disappear into the government's purse and being at the mercy of their spending decisions, most of us can support the idea that by paying taxes we all get to benefit. There is a sense of supporting the overall good. And I'll be honest, I do not fancy being responsible for my own street lighting wherever I go. Total chore.

Now that we have agreed that taxation is a good idea, let's break it down into categories and look at the different types of tax we pay, how they are collected and what they do with that money.

What Types of Tax Are There Then?

Dusting off my A level in economics here to give you a bit of a beginner's guide to tax, and it was a long time ago that I sat that exam, so bear with.

Tax falls into two broad categories: direct and indirect taxation. Now the former is when they take money directly from you. Good examples of this are income tax and National Insurance. These taxes are the ones that you know about and have a little cry over every payday. They are taxing you on the money that you have made. Businesses get direct tax too, so don't go thinking that they are in some way avoiding that.

Indirect taxes on the other hand are sneakier. It is not like anyone is actually hiding it, but you could easily pay indirect tax and not know. The best example of this is Value Added Tax – VAT. It is this tax that makes me scoff in derision when someone tells me they don't pay tax: 'Er...

you do!' Well, if you buy anything from the shops that is considered a luxury, you do. And it really doesn't take much for something to be considered a luxury – I mean tampons were considered a luxury until 2021.

Let's look at some of the big ones here in the UK and talk a bit about how much you will pay and how that money is collected.

DIRECT TAXES

Income tax

Sometimes called PAYE (Pay As You Earn) tax, this is the government's biggest money-maker. In the year 2022–23 it raised £250 billion towards public spending.[11] Like I said, this is the one that takes money out of your pay. It is largely considered to be a progressive tax, which means that the more you earn the more you pay.

Everyone gets what is called a tax-free allowance, which at the time of writing is £12,570 a year. If you earn under this, you won't have to pay income tax. Even if you earn over this, that first £12,570 is tax-free. After that, it goes up in bands, so the next chunk you earn, to £50,570, is taxed at 20 per cent, then between that and £125,140 at 40 per cent. Any more than that and you are going to lose 45 per cent of it. Now these figures change a lot, so make sure to check out the government website for the latest bands and rates. (https://www.gov.uk/income-tax-rates)

National Insurance contributions

This is the other type of tax that you are going to see on your payslip; but there are a few types of National Insurance. Some paid by employees, some by employers, and some by the self-employed. Largely, it doesn't really matter. You just need to know that however you make money you are probably going to be paying this tax.

Just like income tax, this is largely accepted as a progressive tax; but only up to a point. The more you earn the more you pay, but after around £1,000 a week it gets a bit iffy, with higher earners paying a lower percentage than lower earners. I'll let you decide how you feel about that one.

Other types of direct taxes that are paid here in the UK include capital gains tax, which is a tax on the sale of assets, and inheritance tax, which you pay on money you get when someone dies. Both are much smaller contributors to the public spending wallet and are typically paid by higher-earning households. That said, if you meet the criteria to pay then there is no chance that you are getting out of it unless you have put some plans in place in advance.

INDIRECT TAXES

Value added tax (VAT)

As the third highest source of income for the government, VAT is a significant money-maker – it brought in £162 billion in 2022–23. As I mentioned before, this is a tax on stuff that you buy. Now there is a list of stuff that you don't have to pay VAT on, including things like kids' clothes, bread, and – strangely – cake. For everything else, VAT is split into two categories: a standard rate, which is currently 20 per cent, and a reduced rate of 5 per cent.

The reduced rate is for selected products such as energy and fuels, children's car seats and even, in some cases, caravans. Some period products are still on this list, period pants being the most notable one, and plenty of people are fighting to change this.

Outside of these products and services, pretty much everything else is charged at the standard rate. Biscuits are taxable, adult clothes are taxable, and even toilet rolls are taxable. This is why I believe that EVERYONE pays tax.

Excise duties

This tax is designed to stop you from buying stuff that could actually be detrimental to society or to government spending. Basically, they want you to buy less of these items, and they use this tax to increase the price if they think that you might be buying too much. The list of these items is alcohol, tobacco, gambling products and fuels.

While I have covered the big ones here, this is not an exhaustive list. There are lots of other taxes that we pay. I could have mentioned council tax, which goes to the local government and is paid by most people who live in a house. Or I could have chatted about road tax, which is calculated based on the level of CO_2 emissions your vehicle produces. Or insurance premium tax. Or corporation tax. Or dividend tax...

The bottom line is that there are lots of different taxes, and all raise different amounts of money for the government and may or may not have a secondary purpose too, just like with excise duties.

It is practically impossible to not pay tax, and most of the time you won't even know you are paying it. But there are definitely ways that you can pay less.

How to Pay Less Tax – Legally

If you thought I was about to share some shady tactics to help you get out of paying taxes altogether, then I'm afraid that I am going to have to disappoint you. As a form of consolation prize, however, I am willing to share a few tips and tricks that I know to help you pay less tax legally.

Whenever I post a video about this on my social media accounts, there is always some keyboard warrior ready to tell me that it is unethical to encourage people to pay less tax, and I always take great pleasure in telling them to jog on.

One of the beautiful things about living in the age that we do, when we have access to all this information at our fingertips, is that we get to use it. As I am writing this, I am scratching my head wondering how my parents would have gone about learning about the various legal strategies to reduce their tax bill. Did they read about it in the paper? See it on the news? Or did they have to pay out for a financial adviser?

Either way, this is one of the main perks of being of this generation; we can learn this stuff with a quick google and use it to our advantage. It's the consolation prize for not being born in the sixties and experiencing the housing market boom that our parents thrived on.

Anyway, I got a little sidetracked, but the point stands that these strategies are literally created by the government to help us out. Plus, the government normally gives some sort of motive too. In essence, you aren't going to catch me feeling bad about doing any of these and I fully intend to tell as many people about them as I can, starting with you.

TAX CODES

One of the best things that you can do is to make sure that your tax code is correct. This is a little number and a letter, and it appears on your tax slip and tells your employer what you need to pay in tax. Normally it is accurate, but everyone I have ever known has dealt with an incorrect tax code at some point.

One of the most common times for your tax code to go wrong is when you start a new job. If you haven't passed on your P45 or there is something complicated about your tax situation it can cause some issues. Therefore, it is worth checking your tax code. If you suspect that it is wrong, then give HMRC a ring.

There's more.

There are ways in which you can change your tax code to reflect some of your expenses, even as an employee. This is called tax relief. The best example of this is if you need to wear a uniform for your job. If this is you, then you can apply to have your tax code changed to claim back some of the costs of cleaning the company-issued uniform at home. There's even more good news here though, and that is that you can backdate this for up to four years previous. So if you've been wearing a uniform to work and washing it at home, then you could be entitled to get some money back in your pocket. Ker-ching!

Another example of this is if you are a member of a professional organisation. I learned about this one as a teacher, because (obviously) I was in a union. You can't claim back the full cost of membership, but you can claim back the tax you would have paid on it. Again, this is a type of tax relief and can be backdated.

There are lots of other ways that you can claim tax relief as an employee. They include if you work from home, or if you use a car for work, or a whole host of other things. Even if you don't think that you will be able to claim this tax relief, it is always worth a check. Hell, you might be pleasantly surprised.

MARRIAGE TAX ALLOWANCE

I love this one as it is one that I have personally taken advantage of over the years. It is not for everyone, but it could save you a couple of hundred pounds in tax. I wouldn't say no to that if it was on offer.

In order to be able to benefit from this you typically need to fulfil two main criteria. Firstly you have to be married or in a civil partnership, and secondly one of you needs to be earning below the income tax personal allowance threshold. There are several reasons that this might happen. One of you might be a stay-at-home parent, working part-time or perhaps on parental leave. It doesn't even have to be a permanent situation; you just need to earn below the threshold in one particular year.

It is worth reviewing this if one of you has been out of work or working reduced hours for any particular reason in any tax year. It is the responsibility of the person who is below the threshold to 'gift' their spare allowance to their partner. Unfortunately, you cannot share your entire allowance, just a part of it, but it is still better than nothing at all.

ISAS

Individual Savings Accounts, or ISAs, are the crème de la crème of tax savings strategies and if you are not utilising them then you are majorly missing out. Every UK adult has access to £20,000 worth of tax-free savings or investments every year, but data says that only 61 per cent of UK adults actually have an ISA account.[12]

Whaaattt?

I get that not everyone has savings or investments that they feel are enough to need an ISA account, but, given that they are free, I say why not get one anyway? What's the harm (even if there's not much money in it)?

What is an ISA then? Well, I will cover this in more detail in Chapter Seven (along with all types of savings accounts); but, simply put, they are a type of savings account that allows you to earn interest or achieve capital growth and not have to pay tax on any of it. Most savings outside of one of these accounts – not all – will be subject to tax on any interest earned, because it is money made and the government wants their cut. But they do want to encourage you to save, so they provide these accounts with this nice little incentive to get you to think about it more.

ISAs really come into their own, however, when you look at the stocks and shares versions, where you can invest your money and not have to worry about paying dividend tax or capital gains tax on any money made in this way. Over a period of several years, this could be a significant amount of money.

If you are going to save or invest, then it would be wise to consider looking into ISAs first, because then you can pay less tax and that's the point of this chapter eh?

BUSINESSES

One aspect that we haven't spoken much about in this chapter is tax relating to businesses, the reason being that this is primarily a personal finance book; but as we are covering things such as self-employment I will touch upon this briefly here.

If you are running your own business, then one of the best things you can do if you want to ensure that you are being as tax efficient as possible is to get yourself a decent accountant. They will be able to advise you on the actions you can specifically take to achieve your tax goals.

Even if you are currently acting as a sole trader, you may want to speak to an accountant if you are seeing an increase in your turnover and want to make smart tax decisions. It might be that there are better options for how you can run your business, and of course you want to set up your business in a certain way to achieve the best tax efficiency for you and your family.

If you've managed to make it this far, then give yourself a bloody great pat on the back. A whole section on tax was always going to be a bit of a slog, but I refuse to let you exist in the world of money without at least having a grasp of the basic concepts of tax. And if there is a tax saving to be had, I want you to know about that too. Knowledge is money.

Chapter Five

Sorting Out Your Spending

If there is one thing that I do well, it is wasting my money on crap that I don't need or even particularly want. Honestly, this is a skill that I am so competent in that there is a small part of me that wonders how I haven't been called upon to do it professionally yet.

My first experience of wasting money comes from about 20 years ago. Sixteen-year-old me found myself down the high street one Saturday with my bestie from school with £30 on my Solo card and not a clue what I wanted to spend it on, but determined to get it out of my bank account at the fastest speed possible.

Obviously, this wasn't exactly what I was thinking. Instead, I was thinking, 'Oh my God! I need these silver contact lenses.' Yep! You read that correctly. Silver contact lenses. I swear the bloke on the desk at Argos was having a right giggle as he handed those over to me. I mean I was a massive nerd back then too, so I reckon he was probably creasing as he pictured me in my flared jeans and silver contact lenses.

Anyway, you can imagine the earful I got off my mum

when I returned home with, and I quote, 'That load of pointless crap!' After an eternity of a lecture that included her telling me that if I wore them I was going to ruin my eyes, she insisted I wore them to 'get my money's worth.' So that night I rocked up to my mate's sixteenth-birthday sleepover looking like some futuristic alien that had been experimenting with illegal substances. Oh, and they made my eyes hurt. Needless to say, they went in the bin about an hour after I arrived.

Despite the trauma of this contact lens event, I did not learn my lesson. I spent another 15 years or so grappling with spending and figuring out what was a good use of my money and what wasn't. Even now, there are still times when I am disappointed with my choices, but I have learned to be kinder to myself about them, so that is progress too, I think.

The thing is that there has never been a time in history when there are so many demands on your hard-earned cash and also so much encouragement to waste it. My parents were also victims of a world where they were encouraged to spend their money. You'd read the newspaper and there would be an advert for some crockery with Princess Diana's face on it for a bargain price. Or on the drive to work there would be an ad for cigarettes on a billboard opposite the traffic lights. (I know! The fact that they were allowed to advertise for cigarettes still blows my mind too.)

But millennials and Gen Z, as well as growing up with that, now have to contend with targeted ads too. Every electronic device in our home is now listening to every twitch, fart and conversation and recommending us products and services as a result. If I so much as even mention that I like my mate's scarf near an Alexa, I'll spend the rest of the week fending off adverts on every social media platform showing me a range of shockingly similar scarves. Like can Alexa see too?!

As I write this, the whole world seems to find itself in a cost of living crisis. Inflation is through the roof and wages aren't catching up quickly enough. The result is that we are being forced to spend more of our money but we still get the same amount, or sometimes even less, stuff. Not cool cozzie livs.

So, in case earning the money wasn't more challenging than ever, you have to figure out the tax thingy, and now you have to figure out what to spend your money on. This is the beautiful and terrifying part of money management that no one particularly wants to face, but it has to be done.

What to Spend Your Money On

As much as it would be de-bloody-lightful to get paid and just be like, 'What shall I spend this money on?', unfortunately it rarely works out like that. Instead, I'd wager the majority of your income will be spent on purely existing in a state of relative comfort. You'll have to spend it on your mortgage or rent, then council tax (remember that from Chapter Five?), then gas and electricity and water, and then food.

This list so far is very similar to the expenses that my parents would have had to pay for at my age. But our list doesn't stop there. Broadband is now considered an essential service, so we are paying for that too. Mobile phone contracts are also coming out of that. Chances are you have some sort of travel expenses too. Not saying that boomers didn't have cars. They did. However, they were likely bought outright or via a loan, but now it is pretty much normal to have cars on some form of payments scheme and many don't even result in ownership. Fuel is more expensive than ever. Oh and, if you are using public transport, that's more expensive as well.

And, if pure survival isn't quite your cup of tea, then you might want to stick a few luxuries in the spending mix too.

Some luxuries are barely luxuries these days and more like premium essentials. I am talking about things like Netflix, Amazon Prime and Spotify. Tell someone you don't have one of these and they'll look at you like you've just sprouted a second head. Plus, they are considered the minimum in entertainment. If in doubt, you can always shove on a Netflix series to binge-watch and help you forget about the rest of your problems.

I've not even started to mention the costs that you might incur if you have kids. There's school uniforms, school trips, school bake sales, that weird travelling bookshop that comes round to schools once a year, after-school clubs, friends' birthday parties – and all on top of keeping them alive too.

Oh and now you need insurance for everything too!

Pets? You'll need insurance! Car? House? Obviously need insurance. Going on holiday? Insurance! Mobile phone? Yep. Insurance. Don't wanna break it and have to go back to your mum's old iPhone 1. Laptop? Probably should. Breakdown cover? Yeah, you'll need that. In case you die? Get some for that. No NHS dentist? Best get health insurance then. What if you are critically ill? Suppose you need that too.

Don't get me wrong, I know that kids and insurance existed for our folks too. But there are increasing numbers of ways that these things cost us money. It never ends.

And there's nothing enjoyable about having insurance. It's pretty much like assuming the worst and spending all your money on the expectation of it happening. Sure, there's a sense of peace of mind and I fully support having it. But wow is it a boring use of money!

After all of this, you might find yourself in the fortunate position of having a bit left over. This is the bit that you choose to spend on what you want. But how do you know what to spend it on?

You could, of course, choose to save it or invest it. Those chapters are coming, I promise. But for the sake of this chapter on spending, how do you spend it meaningfully rather than feeling that flood of regret later?

The key is to remember what you want. You've already done a lot of work in this area earlier in the book. You need to have a clear concept of what you do and don't want in your life and align your spending with this.

Let me give you some indication of what I mean by that.

If your lifelong goal is to travel the world, then you shouldn't spend your money on household gadgets and clutter that you are going to have to sell or store when you head off. Firstly, because that money you spent on those items could be of better use in your savings account to fund that trip of a lifetime, and secondly you are reaffirming to yourself that you want a house full of things, not a life of freedom.

Another example? Okay! Maybe you have a dream of running your first marathon? Then how about spending your money on decent running shoes. You could also buy books telling inspirational stories by other marathon runners, or join a running club. It is not always about what you shouldn't be spending your money on, but sometimes about what you should.

The point is that spending your money is not an inherently evil activity. In fact, you should be able to spend your money on things that bring you joy and support the lifestyle that you want to live. We are not going to admonish ourselves for buying tickets to see Harry Styles if our lifelong goal is to see Harry Styles. In my opinion, that's what you should be spending your money on. Mission accomplished!

What is needed is discretion. Buying running shoes because everyone is doing Parkrun but you're more of a swimmer is wasteful. Buying Harry Styles tickets because of FOMO is also wasteful. Those pointless household gadgets that lure you in until you remember you don't care about making your own pasta? Wasteful.

This is unique and personal to you. You cannot let

someone else tell you what is or isn't a waste of your money. You need to sit and work that out for yourself.

Now, the caveat to this purposeful spending is that you can't neglect your basic responsibilities. This little spending adventure started with me telling you that you need to cover the whole basic-existing thing first. You gotta pay those bills. Sorry to be boring but you do. It doesn't matter what you've bought to make your dreams come true if your landlord is evicting you and you've got no heating in December.

But, conversely, we are not going to spend our whole lives clinging to a vision of what we want for our retirement. I refuse to advocate for putting our dreams on hold until some magical day in the future. If there is action we can take to make them happen now, then we can and should use our money accordingly. Let's be bold – but within the realms of being responsible towards ourselves and our loved ones. I promise that, if you want to make it happen, there is space in your finances for both.

How to Avoid Temptation

At some point in early 2020, I found myself in some Airbnb in Eastern Europe downloading TikTok and rapidly messaging a couple of my business besties in our group WhatsApp. After a long time of being a classic millennial and refusing to jump on what looked like a social media platform for Gen Z, I had been encouraged to 'give it a go' and see what the fuss was about.

I was, unknowingly, nearing the end of my time travelling the world, and during this trip I had managed to live a blissfully simple life. My family and I had decided before we left that we would only travel with hand luggage. The result of this was that I had one medium-sized backpack and then essentially a handbag to fit everything I needed in for that indefinitely long trip. (If you need it in terms of weight, I was carrying 7.2 kilos and that included my laptop.)

It was a dream!

Doing laundry was an easy-peasy task because I only had a handful of clothes to wash. Packing up every time we moved took minutes. Jumping on flights was a doddle because we had all our stuff with us all the time. There was no losing or misplacing things because there was so little to watch over that I knew where it was at all times.

I had never been one to consider minimalist living, but travel life had me converted. It was a weight off my shoulders. Less stuff = less stress, and I'll argue that until hell freezes over.

The other beauty of this situation was that my bag was packed with absolute precision. I had zero chance of squeezing a single extra thing in there, let alone some crappy souvenir that caught my eye. Buying stuff was basically out of the question.

Don't get me wrong, I did buy one or two things, but these were normally replacements for items that were worn out. For example, we somehow managed to lose the girls' cardigans in a hospital in Peru. So you can imagine my delight when I realised this meant we could go shopping for brightly coloured, pint-sized alpaca-wool jumpers. Best day ever. On top of that, I did treat myself to the odd anklet or pair of earrings as these were small and could be worn on the plane instead of needing to be packed into a suitcase.

Despite all of this, however, it was a lesson for me in avoiding all the temptation. And you can bet there was A LOT of temptation. But knowing that I couldn't take the items with me meant that I was happy to say no to buying them in the first place. Remarkably, over time I found myself less tempted in general. I wouldn't get sucked in by the street vendors or flap my hands in delight at every souvenir shop.

What I did in lieu of buying memories was that I participated in them instead. I pointed out the sights, the sounds and the smells to my children. I cheered and danced and sang along with street performers. I jumped in oceans, rivers and lakes. And melted at the delight on my children's faces when they saw a parrot fly past or a giant bat in a tree.

This all makes me sound like a walking cliché, but I genuinely believe that, if you can remove the urge to constantly spend money or to be suckered into the temptation of parting with your cash, then suddenly the world is a little bit more interesting. The need to spend almost feels like a preoccupation: 'What can I buy next?'

Think about this. If I say I'll give you £50 right now, what are your first thoughts? I bet for most people reading this you've got a mental shopping list and are weighing up the merits of each item. There is a constant societal nagging that tells us that money should be spent – you need this and if you get it now your life will be better.

Now, going back to TikTok. Little did I know back then that I would be downloading yet another platform that was going to be tempting me to buy more stuff. I mean if I'd have properly thought about it I would have known, but I was just curious to see what the hype was all about.

Four years on from that Airbnb app downloading sesh, I now have a list of things in my head that I want from TikTok. Hell, I'll even confess to having bought a couple of them. (No-heat curlers and rosemary oil if you must know.)

The temptation is everywhere. It is on billboards and TV and in newspapers in the same way that it was for the generations before us, but it is also on our phones, laptops, game consoles and smart devices. It is unavoidable, but not unovercomeable.

The first tip is to limit your exposure to this temptation. This might sound easier said than done, but it can be simple actions such as unsubscribing from marketing emails. We all know that, even when we aren't in the market for something, a cheeky 40 per cent off email can have us taking a look anyway.

You can go further with this and avoid physical shops altogether. I'm a big fan of having a mooch around the city, but can I be trusted to do this and not find my purse opening and my debit card leaping out ready to purchase something I didn't know I needed? Nope! If I want to go for a walk or get out of the house, I'll head to the woods or the beach instead.

Those apps on your phone for Vinted, eBay, Amazon, Shein and whoever else – you can delete those too. As a billy bonus, this will set you free from the notifications offering you discounts on your next shop too. Also further temptation.

Another great strategy is to shop with purpose aka write a shopping list. Your nan has been doing this for years and you probably have too, but build up further discipline around this practice and, if it ain't on the list, you ain't buying it. That is that. Supermarkets and high street stores are all packed with clever marketing tactics designed to lure you and have you buying all the random toot that you don't need.

Make a list and stick to it!

And finally on this one, tempt yourself with something else. Fill your life with reminders of what you do actually want. I'm talking lock-screen photos of that villa on the Italian coast, or vision boards at the end of your bed that flood your mind with images of the life you are chasing. Heck! I've even gone as far as Sellotaping a picture to my credit card to act as a deterrent. Be tempted by the real temptations, like early retirement, world travel and home ownership.

Here's a fun little story about this. One day I realised I was a little bit addicted to caramel-sweetened iced coffees. I mean I stand by this, they're delicious. But at over £5 a time, they were damaging not just my pancreatic function but also my bank account. So I decided that every time I wanted one and didn't have one I would stick £5 into my investment account.

Now I probably wanted them even more that month because I never got to satiate the urge, but I ended up investing £70. Later on in this book you'll learn all about how that £70 wasn't actually £70 saved but much more than that. But at the bottom of this little coffee-related tale is the idea that, if you offer yourself something better, you can avoid all manner of other temptations.

Tackling Overspending

I have worked with a lot of people as a financial coach over the years and nearly all of them have said that they spend too much money. Overspending is a massive problem for a lot of households in the UK. The Office for National Statistics has found that even pre-Covid, 65 per cent of households were spending more than their income on a monthly basis.[13] That's shocking!

But also not completely unexpected. As I have said, so many people struggle with this and consequently find themselves battling financial stress, dealing with debt, and just feeling like a bit of failure when it comes to money. But you have to remember that your entire experience of life is basically pushing you to buy more stuff. It's not your fault! That said, this doesn't mean that there is nothing you can do about it.

You've already got a few tricks on dealing with temptation up your sleeve by now, so you don't have much more work to do to tackle your overspending.

Before we get into that, though, let's look at some of the root causes of overspending. The first is that we aren't getting paid enough. Right now, the cost of living crisis is the number one reason why people are struggling. Things cost too much and our wages aren't going up quickly enough. You can't put that on you.

Back when I started chatting about money on the interwebs, I was telling people a very different set of rules. It was 'cut your spending, switch your energy supplier, sack off Sky and sort your life out.' Yet here we are six years on and that feels cruel now. But there is still a hint of hope within it.

We've already gone over how you can get paid and seek out the best-paid jobs that you can. This is hugely important. I mean like this might be the most important thing that you read in this book: MAKE MORE MONEY. Yeah, I can tell you all week how to save money and cut your spending, but I wouldn't have to if you made more money.

Simplistic?

No, it's not! Even if you feel like getting a higher-paying job is a challenge for you, there are still options. Go back to the getting-paid chapter. There are a million ways you could make more money and therefore keep spending just as you do now. And the real perk of this solution is that there is no upper limit on how much money you can make. You could become the richest person in the world and keep making more. No one is going to pop out of the woodwork and be like, 'Righto, that's enough money for you!'

Conversely, when you look at cutting your spending, then perhaps you'll find some magical way of never spending money again, and what have you achieved? An extra couple of grand in your pocket a month? I mean that's bloody decent, but it ain't no richest human to have ever existed.

Choose how you spend your time on this wisely.

Buuuuutttt... you could probably still benefit from reining in the spending and cutting back a bit. No harm in that eh? Plus, it is a cracking skill to have up your sleeve for a rainy day. So why not get some practice in now?

Start by looking back at your bank statements from the last few months. If you have a banking app that provides you with graphs and summaries of your spending, then this is going to save you a lot of work. Because I want you to see where your money is going. After you have taken out all the stuff you need to spend money on, what is happening to the rest?

It's these leaks that are going to sink your ship, as they say. It will be the odd iced coffee here and there, or the trip to Primark, or the beauty subscription box whose contents you don't even use. These things add up. It's not to say that some of this might not be a part of what you really want to be spending your money on. Ignore those things for now. Instead, focus your efforts on plugging the leaks that are for things you weren't sure you wanted anyway. Use the temptation tricks a few pages back to help you.

Back to those needs! They don't get off scot-free. You can make them cost less too. If anything, I would say that there is more that you can do here, because these are normally your biggest expenses. Take your mortgage, for example. When your fixed term ended, did you speak to a broker and get yourself the best deal on the market? Nope? Well, go do that and see how much you might save.

Look at your utility bills too. Are you on a decent tariff? Yeah, it might still be expensive, but at least let's not overpay on this one. Mobile phones! Do you really need a new one every couple of years? Probably not. I stopped getting new phones regularly and switched to SIM-only contracts, and saved myself a small fortune.

We will talk more about debt later, but this could be a big area where you could spend less money. Maybe a balance transfer on a credit card to a 0 per cent deal could help you cut back your outgoings. Or perhaps you need to talk to someone about debt affordability and if you can really even manage this at all.

To summarise this section, when it comes to overspending you need a double-ended approach: make more and spend less. If you make this a priority, then I promise you that it won't be long before you start seeing the fruits of your labours. Your spending will settle down and your income will creep up, and suddenly you'll realise that you aren't as stressed about money as you were. It's worth the effort. I promise.

The Power of Marketing

Before I move away from this chapter on spending, I thought I would talk to you a little bit about marketing and how it is influencing you to spend your money. I have mentioned this a bit throughout the previous chapters, but I wanted to drill deeper into what is going on and help you recognise what is happening to you.

The thing is, you are being marketed to ALL. THE. TIME.

Pretty much every interaction you have with your phone, your computer, or out in the world will leave you exposed to some sort of marketing.

Back in 2021, I decided to learn more about marketing. Despite my writing about how you should be on the lookout for marketing, my business is basically all about marketing. Therefore, it was beneficial for me to study for it, and in early 2022 I gained a degree-equivalent qualification in the subject. It was eye-opening.

There are whole teams of people working for pretty much every corporation in the world to get you to buy stuff. And they know all about you. Plus, they have an entire toolbox of tricks that they can employ to get you part with your cash.

Take the supermarket. The place is designed to get you to spend the maximum amount of money possible. The first step you take through the door will be subjecting you to years' worth of marketing research all piled onto the floor.

Think about what you are most likely to go to the shop

for – milk? Bread? And where do you find those products in most supermarkets? Typically, one of them is at the far corner of the shop and the other is buried somewhere in the middle. This forces you to walk past dozens of other aisles of offers and treats to get to what you went in there for.

If you were designing a supermarket for pure convenience and ease of use, you would probably put the bread and milk right next to the door, right? Followed immediately by a self-service checkout, so you could grab and go without all that temptation. But temptation is precisely what they are working on.

Clothes, seasonal items and other random stuff like cherry-flavoured vodka are normally found near the front of the store. With loads of posters that talk about what an amazing deal it is. No one 'pops in' for any of that stuff, but I bet you think, 'You know what? I'll just have a little look around the clothes while I'm here. And I best grab some of that vodka while it's on offer!'

We all do it!

Even the blooming meal deals are creeping further and further back. One supermarket near me moved their 'to-go' food right to the back of the supermarket. Others made me walk past all the clothes and books to get there. It's great for my daily step count, but after I'd picked up a new belt and a bestseller on the way to pick up my lunch my bank account was groaning.

But it goes deeper than this.

I think we are well aware that the end aisles are designed to draw us in. The amount of cheese I have purchased over the years because it was on an end aisle would probably make me cry if I ever saw that number written down. And yeah, the food looks great. Particularly during BBQ season, when those 3-for-£10 deals crop up and make you think you've nabbed the bargain of your life on kebab skewers.

It's not just those pesky end aisles you need to watch out for though. The standard aisles are full of marketing tricks too. Did you know that they put the products with the higher profit margins at eye level? This is so that when you are looking you are instantly drawn to them. But if you look above or below instead, then you might find some serious deals. If you don't believe me, go and take a look around your nearest supermarket.

But it is not exclusively the supermarkets that are using the power of marketing to ensnare you. All the shops are doing it, whether they are physical stores or online.

Let's have a chat about the latter.

Alphabet, the parent company of Google, is the leading global advertiser. In 2022, they saw ad revenues of approximately $225.5 billion[14] practically double the revenues of the second-place holder, Meta: aka Facebook, Instagram and WhatsApp. Amazon took third place, in case you are wondering. This just shows that some of the biggest and most successful companies are making money from helping smaller businesses to get you to buy stuff. This isn't even the money they make from selling to you directly. It's a serious industry.

Back to Google then: one of the reasons that Google is so accomplished at advertising is because they know all about you. If you head to your Google account and visit 'Data and Privacy' and then 'Personalised Ads', you will be able to see all the personal details that they have on you.

When I had a look at mine, it knew my age, my marital status, that I was a homeowner, my education level and what industry I worked in – but it didn't think I had kids, so have it Google! Ha! You can bet it knows a lot more than that too. It knows your likes and dislikes, where you've been and where you wanna go next. It knows where you live and where you work, what you do for fun and things you hate.

And it takes all this information and uses it to sell you stuff.

You cannot avoid it.

I know I am not alone in getting weirdly creeped out when I get an advert pop-up after I have had a random conversation about something. The social etiquette here is to tell the other person that it was weird and follow up with, 'They're listening!' We joke. But they are.

Every little click, scroll and linger on the internet provides some advertising and marketing team with information about you, and they use that to steer you towards their products. One of the basic principles I learned about marketing in my course was STP – Segmentation, Targeting and Positioning.

All the data that search engines, social media and whatnot collect about you allows them to group us into categories. For example, Google knows my age and gender, so they will lump me together with other women of my age and look to flog me stuff like anti-ageing creams and home workout equipment. (It works! I have both!). But different companies will group you according to different reasons that benefit them.

The next step is targeting. Not every industry wants to sell something to you. Phew! Or at least not right now. So what they do is choose groups to focus on. That anti-ageing cream company might go for women in their thirties who like a sunny holiday and share their pictures on Instagram as their starting point. Because then they can start to tailor their product and marketing towards that person. This is positioning.

This whole cycle goes on and on, over and over, splitting people into different categories and changing their products to suit different audiences. Coca-Cola does this well. Take Diet Coke; they focused on women who want to enjoy the product but want to stay in shape. But when they realised men wanted this too, but found Diet Coke too girly, they launched Coke Zero. The manly Coke!

So why am I telling you all this?

Well, I want you to know that all this voodoo marketing science is a whole new level of challenge that you have to navigate that your nan did not. If you find yourself more easily sucked into buying stuff, it's because of the world that you live in. It is designed to be like that.

But also, I want you to notice it. To look out for it. When you start to recognise that this happens to you, then you can sidestep out of the process. This could look like switching off those personalised ads on Google, unsubscribing from those marketing emails, or bypassing those huge promotions at the supermarket entrance.

No person can jump off the marketing hamster wheel completely, but you can spot when you might be being sucked in. If you stop yourself from getting dragged into just one pointless and shallow purchase because you spotted the marketing stuff that was happening to you, then this section has achieved its mission.

It's a wild world out there and it is trying to take all your money. Good luck!

Chapter Six

To Buy or Not to Buy

I feel the need to take a deep breath for this one. It is a massively loaded and divisive topic that seems to have become an obsession for society at large. As you get swept along in the current of money-related advice, it seems that your thoughts and feelings on whether or not you want to buy a house are irrelevant. Everyone else is doing it so you should too.

As a twenty-something I felt the same pressure. I had watched many of my colleagues who were my age purchase their first homes. I was saving my butt off and could not fathom how they were managing to do it just a couple of years after finishing university. Was it inheritances? Were they significantly out-earning me?

In my head, I had always assumed that I would buy a house. It was what my parents and grandparents had done as soon as they could afford to, and I should do the same too. Somewhat rebelliously, and after several long hard years of saving, I bought a house and moved in with my then-boyfriend and later-husband, even though we weren't married or even engaged. It wasn't how my family did things, but progress eh?

There is a part of me that looks back and can't really believe that we were able to afford it. It was a lot of money, but bloody hell was it cheaper then than it is now. See, back then the average house price was £157,600, and we bought our three-bed end of terrace for less than that. The average salary back then was £26,000; approximately one-sixth of the average house price.

Fast forward ten years and at time of writing the average house price is £277,000, which means it has close to doubled in that ten-year period. Now this isn't unexpected, and it follows the general trend for house prices. What is more important in this scenario is what has happened to the average salary.

If your arithmetic skills are any good, then you will probably have worked out that to match the increases in house prices the average UK salary should be at least £50k. At this point, you might be crying into your payslip and wondering what happened. What happened was that salaries have not kept pace with house prices.

The average UK salary (for a full-timer) is just over £31,000. Yep! A £5,000 increase in ten years – or just over 20 per cent, compared to the 78 per cent increase in the average house price. Not exactly keeping up. Or, to put it another way, average salaries are now just one-ninth of the average house price. A fairly significant drop!

The point I am trying to make here is that house prices have increased at a faster rate than our salaries. Meaning that, in real terms, houses are more expensive. They require more of our money to buy, and consequently more hours of work for most of us.

What's more is that this is just what has happened in the last ten years. This is the experience of one millennial who lucked out and bought in the house price dip after the 2008–09 recession. Trust me when I say I know we were bloody lucky.

The question I regularly find myself trying to answer is: if saving for a deposit back in 2012 was hard, what on Earth would it be like now? I mean we scraped the 10 per cent together, and that was by using some of my student loans that I had been stashing in a high-interest savings account while working 15 to 20 hours a week through uni to make ends meet. Oh, and I had my golden hello of £5,000 for becoming a teacher. They taxed it though, so I got about £3.5k in the end. I raged!

Even with all that privilege carrying me up the house deposit stream, it was still bloody hard. I don't even know if we would be able to do it now. Would a 23-year-old teacher and her retail team leader boyfriend be able to save a 10 per cent deposit on a £250,000 house?

The point to all that is to say, 'I get it!' It was crap then and it is double crap now.

But it does open up a broader question: should you even bother buying?

Now this is the question that you should be asking. Most people jump straight in by asking, 'How can I buy a house?' This is great, but you are missing out on a lot of the steps. This chapter will help you to pause and reflect on whether or not buying property is the right move for you. I don't think that there are any other investments that people are so willing to throw their money at without pondering the risks and returns first.

Pros and Cons, Risks and Costs

I could name dozens of people who have wandered casually into home ownership because they 'gotta get a foot on the property ladder' or 'you're wasting money renting' or 'it's the best investment'. Yet I am not sure any of them have picked up a calculator to do the maths.

I mean I am people too.

My parents said home ownership was good. My nan said home ownership was good. They had done all right out of it, so why wouldn't I?

Here is the thing. The boomers actually aren't okay. I mean some of them obviously are, but there are huge numbers that are in a bit of a pickle now. There is a similar picture among the older generations too.

Many are what is described as Asset Rich Cash Poor (ARCP), which means that a lot of their money is stuck in stuff. Most significantly their houses. As incomes drop in retirement and the cost of living increases, many pensioners are left battling with the idea of selling the roof over their heads to cover their bills. Not fun!

One study by the Institute of Chartered Accountants Scotland[15] found that this group of people – particularly the women among them – had done very little financial planning earlier in their lives. They had most of their wealth sunk into their property but, due to downturns in the stock market and low savings rates, weren't in the position they had hoped to be in at this point.

The lesson in all of this is that perhaps considering a property an investment is not the best approach. Particularly when you can't buy food with a house and everyone needs a roof over their head.

A great starting point for the property debate is to decide whether you consider it an investment or a home. Or is it possible for it to be both?

Let's take a look at what we require from a home:

- Warm
- Dry
- Located near people you care about
- Enough space
- Pleasing decor
- Comfortable

For the purpose of comparison, you need to think about what you would want from an investment:

- Increases in value
- Pays you an income

It doesn't have to do both of those, but to be considered an investment it should do one as a minimum. Now I am assuming for the purpose of this exercise that you are going to live in it and not rent it out (I'll talk more about that option later, but the mathematician in me feels the need to lay down some rules before I go into the details.)

For your home to be an investment it needs to increase in value. I started this chapter by saying that house prices are soaring up and up, so this should be a sure thing. Right? Well, maybe not! You see, there are other costs involved with purchasing and maintaining a house, over and above the massive deposit you have to save for. Here is a quick list, plus the rough costs for that average £277k home:

- Stamp duty (£0 for first-time buyers (FTBs), but 5 per cent is payable on anything between £250k and £925k normally)
- Mortgage arrangement fees (£0–£2,500; normally lower interest rates mean higher fees)
- Solicitor fees (£800–£1,500)
- Land registry fee (£300 ish)
- Valuations and surveys (£300 for the valuation and up to £1,500 for additional surveys)
- Moving costs (~£300, but more if you have more stuff)
- Furniture and decoration (how long is a piece of string?)

Just buying the bloody thing is expensive (that's without the costs of maintenance and management) and you pay most of this before you even get the keys. Most people wouldn't factor some of the above into the costs of purchasing their home, but they are in need of consideration. You will have to pay these costs again if you move, and the chances are that you will pay more next time as you will have an estate agent's fee to cover, and more stamp duty. It is normal for people to want to move house later in life to gain more space, get closer to the good schools, move for work, or because they want to live by the sea.

On top of these costs, you will have the ongoing costs of being a homeowner. This is the bit that homeowners normally forget and where renters start to get a bit smug. What additional, ongoing costs might you have? Well, you need to maintain the place, for starters. A fair figure for this in the housing industry is 1 per cent of the property price per year, which for a £277,000 home is around £2,770. And that will go up as the house increases in value.

Then there's insurance.

Buildings, contents and mortgage life. Each will depend on your personal circumstances and the property, but it wouldn't be unreasonable to spend £250–500 a year on these three insurances. If you are a leaseholder, then you may also have to pay a service charge of between £100 and £200 a month.

At this point I feel like I have numerical diarrhoea, so I'll wrap this up and make my point. In the UK, the average monthly rent is £1,060. The monthly mortgage payment on the average house is around the same at £1,080, but when you include all the other stuff it works out at around an additional £400 ish a month. This makes your monthly outgoings for home ownership more like £1,480.

I can hear you say, 'But but but at least I am not wasting my money.' Sure! I hear you!

Let's say that you rent instead. Then take that £400 a month and invest it in the stock market. Given a modest return of 7 per cent annually over 25 years (just like that mortgage term), you'd have £313,000 in the bank. I'll explain this more in the investing chapter, so, if you are confused, hold your horses.

Like with most things money-related, nothing is straightforward. Investing in the stock market is a risk. Buying property is also a risk. Take the mug we bought our first house off. He ended up selling it to us at a loss. The guy bought the place in 2007 right at the peak of the housing market and then watched it crash over the next few years. Poor bloke tried to wait it out by renting the place out for a few years, but eventually sold it to us in 2012, leaving himself over £20,000 out of pocket. It is an investment. It has risks! You might lose money.

Now that we've laid out the costs a bit, when it comes to the buy/not buy debate you need to look at the other elements. Do you actually want to buy a house?

The whole idea behind this book is to present an alternative to the mainstream money management books that exist out there. I am here to shake things up and say, 'Why are we still doing things like that?'

So why ARE we still assuming that home ownership is a rite of passage? Why are we assuming that we want to pick a place and live there forever? Why are we assuming that people want to do DIY for the rest of their lives? Why? Why? Why?

I had this moment the other day. It happens a lot, if I am honest. I turn into a teenager and start shouting,

'It's not fair' and my curse words get super creative. It is quite impressive. I'm proud of them anyway. The reason behind this is that I cannot understand WHY I am living in a three-bed house in the arse end of nowhere Norfolk when I could be living on a beach in Central America.

This isn't some unrealistic fantasy either. It's not like I have dreams above my station. I have travelled the world with my husband and two kids and spent approximately £2,000 a month. Yup! Accommodation, food, travel and entertainment for £2k ish a month. At the time I did this, I had just jumped ship on my teaching career and my financial education business was still a baby. It wasn't going to cover those costs. But now? Hell yeah, it could cover those costs. It could cover those costs and then some. We could sort accommodation from lowest to highest and scroll down a bit.

So why am I living in the arse end of nowhere Norfolk in a three-bed terrace?

There are beaches, beautiful beaches, around the world. Norfolk ain't getting close to the world's best beach list. Why am I here?

This is where my house is. I have a mortgage and bills and stuff. You read the story about how I felt like I drifted into home ownership in my twenties. At the time it was the right thing to do. My job was here, my boyfriend and his family. The plan was job, house, marriage, kids, save. I didn't know any different.

But do I want a house now? I am not so sure.

On the one hand, home ownership provides stability. As long as I pay my mortgage, my family have a roof over their heads. In a few years, maybe sooner, there's a good chance we will be mortgage-free and we will never have to worry about where to live again. My children will never be homeless, and there is a comfort to that.

You might feel the lure of this too. Particularly if you haven't had this stability growing up. You might have moved around a lot as a child, or spent weekends going between your parents' homes. To have a home of your own that no one can take away from you is a comfort. You might want it for your own peace of mind and well-being. That's fine. I'm not here to discourage you from this dream. Instead, it is a dream I want you to pursue and a decision I want you to make consciously.

On reflection, you might find that this static lifestyle is not the one. In fact, you might like the sense of freedom that comes from moving house, location, and even country every six to twelve months. Or maybe even shorter time-frames. Maybe you have a teenager mode that breaks out in a strop every now and then because you aren't on the beach.

Let's face it! Life in the 2020s is better designed for this nomadic lifestyle. Remote working and cheap global travel mean that you can take your job on holiday. The money that would be paying council tax, a mortgage and the gas bill can pay for the apartment with a sea view and a swimming pool.

There could be financial benefits to this too. Back in the early chapters, I said that you can now earn London wages from anywhere in the country thanks to the rise in working from home. This means it is now possible to take home a great salary but live in the cheapest places in the country or the world.

The term for this is geographic arbitrage. You benefit from the lower costs of living in one area to potentially maximise your ability to save or invest – or party. Whatever you fancy really. Of course, it isn't reserved purely for the renters. You could do it with a mortgage too. But I still think that this is a new phenomenon. We are only two years into WFH being a normal and valid way of working, and some people are still nervous about taking the plunge and buying property out of the city centre or away from their place of work. However, I am going to take a guess that this is starting to happen more and more.

Before I move on and give you the low-down on how to buy a house, I want you to pause. Take some time to reflect on your life and lifestyle. Think back to the goals that you set in Chapter Two and where buying a house fits into that. Is it part of the vision? Would it work?

I am totally here for you if you want to buy a house. I just want you to *want* to buy a house. Rather than being caught up in the romanticism of it or because your mum told you so or because your mate got one and now you've got FOMO. Okay? Think about it a bit.

How to Buy a House

This is the part where I tell you how to make buying a house a bit easier. Again, I might be a bit out there with some of my suggestions, but stick with me and you might learn something that helps.

Aside from shortcuts like marrying someone who already has a house or knocking off your parents, there is no simple way to buy a house. For normal people, you are gonna have to spend a good chunk of time saving money before you can start the fun part of looking on Rightmove and eating McDonald's at 10 p.m. outside the house you might put an offer on to 'check the area'.

The good news is that you don't have to go through the process of saving for a house alone. Even if you are single and there's not even a whisper of a potential partner in sight (or perhaps you don't want one). There is support out there that can help you hack the process.

I want to start by looking at the options that are available to help you save. I'm going to cover the process of saving money more fully in the next chapter, so make sure you carry on reading to get all the strategies for where to store your money and get the best returns and whatnot. But there are a couple of savings options that are exclusively for helping people to buy their first home.

LIFETIME ISAS

Have you heard of Lifetime ISAs? This is essentially a tax-free bank account that was introduced in April 2017 to help people with two big savings events in their lives: buying a house and retiring. I'll get to how you can use them for retiring later, but for now you probably want to know how you can use them for buying a house.

LISAs come in two versions. There are cash LISAs, which are savings accounts and on which you can earn interest, and there are stocks and shares versions, which are invested. There are rules about who can open them. You need to be aged between 18 and 40, and you can pay into them until you are 50. But here's the really good bit: the government pays a bonus on whatever you save.

Yep! The government can help you pay for your deposit. This bonus is 25 per cent of whatever you pay in, up to £1,000 a year. Let's take a gander at the numbers then. You pay in £4,000 a year and the government will give you an extra £1,000. That's pretty good, right? I mean if you did that for five years you'd be close to having the 10 per cent deposit on the average house.

But there is further good news. If you are buying a house with someone else, they can also have a LISA and pay in £4,000 a year and get £1,000 in bonuses. There are some rules though. You must both be buying your first property and that property must be worth less than £450,000. You must also have had your LISA open for at least 12 months before you withdraw the money – so, if you are even thinking this might be an option for you, open an account now and stick £1 in.

There are some penalties if you decide to withdraw the money early. It is not unusual for life to change and for you to find that you need to access that money for something. The downside to a LISA is that if you need to access it you'll pay a 25 per cent penalty, which could mean that you lose some of the money that you have put in. I would suggest being pretty clear on whether or not you want to buy a house before you start saving into one of these accounts.

The next question that needs answering is whether should you get a cash or a stocks and shares version. Well, there are a lot of variables in this. The stock market is the riskier option and generally I would only suggest that people look into this option if they are planning a loooooonnggg way ahead. Think ten-plus years. This is because the stock market can go up and down, but over a long time period you can still reasonably expect it to be up from when you started.

With shorter timeframes there is the possibility that, when you need to withdraw the money, you find that the market has dipped below the starting point and you are out of pocket. You don't want that if you have been slogging away to save and now the market has tanked and you have less than you started with.

The consensus is, for short-term savings, like buying a house, stick with the cash option. You won't get a lot of interest on it, but you will still get the bonus. That takes the edge off.

A LISA doesn't have to be the only place that you put your savings; if you are fortunate enough to be able to save more than the annual £4k limit, then you can look at other savings accounts to put this money into. Like I said, next chapter.

But what about if this is all unaffordable still? What if saving enough money for a deposit is out of reach for you? Good news! You still have options.

BUYING TOGETHER

In the past, home ownership was a rite of passage largely for couples. It came somewhere shortly before or after getting married. Now, though, you can buy a house with anyone you like. Multiple people if you want. But it does require serious thought and planning.

A good person you might consider buying a property with is a sibling. Chances are they are a similar age to you and you know a reasonable amount about their financial history and trustworthiness. But you could also consider buying a property with a friend. From the perspective of the mortgage provider, there is no difference between a couple and two siblings or friends purchasing together. You'll need to go through the same affordability checks and you'll have access to the same rates.

This can be a great way to get a foot on the property ladder and start building equity without having the struggle of saving all that money and covering the mortgage on your own. What you do need to be sure of is that the other people you are buying with are financially sound. This includes both their financial history, particularly their credit history as their bad credit score could lower yours too, and their ability to make the mortgage payments in the future.

Now if you want to go down this route then you have a couple of different options for shared ownership. These options are available to everyone even if you are married. You could go down either the joint tenant or the tenants in common route. But what is the difference?

With joint tenants, everyone has equal rights to the property and, when it's sold, equal rights to the profits. It also means that if one of the owners dies then the property automatically passes to the other owners. This is normally fine for married partners and maybe even siblings, but, if you are buying with a boyfriend/girlfriend or a friend, then you may prefer that your share of the property goes to your family if you die.

If this doesn't sound right for you, then you could go for the tenants in common option. This is a good choice if you want to own different shares of the property; for example, it could be that one person can pay more towards the property and therefore wants a larger share. This set-up also means that the other owners don't automatically inherit the property if one person dies. Instead, they have the option to choose what happens to their share in this scenario.

This is actually something that I considered when I bought my first house. I was buying my first property with my boyfriend and I was providing the full deposit. I was weighing up how much I liked this boyfriend and whether I wanted to do unequal shares. I toyed with a 55/45 split to protect the 10 per cent of the property that I had paid for with my deposit. Maybe rather stupidly, I opted for joint tenants, but it worked out in the end because I married him. Ha! But even though I had been with this bloke for five years, I still considered this option, and I urge you to do the same. Don't automatically assume that it will all be okay – think about your wealth too.

There are some not-so-apparent advantages to this

arrangement. If you are the sort of person who craves freedom and flexibility but also doesn't want to miss out on the opportunity to purchase property, then this could be the way to go.

Let's say that two years ago you bought a house with your sister. You enjoy living together, but now you have a job that allows you to travel more and you don't want to be tied to this place that you bought two years ago. Meanwhile, your sister has been dating someone for a couple of years and now wants to move in with them. Divine timing eh?

At this point, you could essentially rent your share of the house out to your sister's partner. They could cover your share of the mortgage and you'd then be free to travel the world and work as you go. You could also come to some arrangement where you still get to keep your room to use when you are back in the country. You just need to make it clear who pays for what, how and when.

What if you haven't got any friends?

Not trying to call you out on anything here, but I don't think that I have any friends that I would consider buying a house with. I do have a sister, and she's a maybe. You might feel that you wouldn't be comfortable buying a property with someone you know and want greater protections in place.

Have you heard of the government's shared ownership scheme? This is designed to help people get on the property ladder if they are unable to save for the full deposit but have the monthly income to cover the bills.

Similarly to buying a property with a friend, relative or partner, you will only need to provide the deposit for part of the house. But you will need to cover the mortgage payments on your share AND pay rent on the share that you don't own. This means that you need to have the monthly income to cover both of these costs, and your mortgage provider will check for this when you make your application.

Like all things, there are rules. Shared ownership is currently only available on new-build homes, or existing shared ownership properties. If you are disabled, however, you might be able to choose a home that suits your needs but doesn't meet the other criteria.

In terms of shares, there are homes that offer 10 per cent ownership, but most are between 25 and 75 per cent. You can also increase your shares through a process known as staircasing, which would lower the amount of rent that you would pay.

Other than this, you can largely treat your home as your own. Structural changes may require written permission from your landlord, who is likely a housing association, your local council or another organisation, but you can decorate and do all the normal house stuff – change the kitchen or the bathroom, put up shelves and do anything else you'd like to do to make it your home.

For people who are living in expensive parts of the country, such as London and the south-east, this scheme is a great way to start the journey to home ownership. You get the perks of buying a house near your family and friends without quite so many years of saving for chunky deposits.

If flexibility is what you crave, though, then this might not be for you.

When my family and I rage-quit on life and went travelling, we decided that we would rent out our house. This would mean that we would have a home to come back to and it would generate a small income as we went. As we were the sole owners of our property, all we needed to do was apply for what is called a 'Consent to Let' through our mortgage provider. This allowed us to rent our house out for 12 months without needing to switch to a different mortgage.

Through the shared ownership scheme, you are allowed to rent out your house, but you still have to be living there. This means that you can invite a friend to live with you to help share the costs, but unless you get permission from your landlord you can't rent it out while you travel. This is typically only given in exceptional situations, such as for members of the military who are serving abroad.

THE NUTS AND BOLTS OF BUYING

Okay! So how do you actually buy a home? How do you get to the stage of looking on Rightmove and eating McDonald's outside the house you might put an offer on?

At this point, I am assuming that you have decided that you want to buy a house, you've decided who you are buying with, how you are going to buy i.e. with your cousin on a tenants in common arrangement, and you've saved your socks off to get the money together to cover both the deposit and the extra home-buying costs. Now you get to the fun part. You get to start the mortgage process.

I also want to tell you about a clueless 24-year-old and her clueless 26-year-old boyfriend who decided to buy a house and they were totally, you guessed it, clueless about the process. That 24-year-old is me.

After getting lots of guidance from the world and her dog, we googled 'how to buy a house' and it told us that to 'unlock' the fun looking-at-houses bit, we needed a decision in principle from our mortgage provider. These are sometimes called agreements in principle, and are basically a certificate that is issued based on your ability to afford a house price. Armed with this, we could start the Rightmove and Zoopla scrolling marathon.

These clueless 20-something-year-olds did find the house they want. There was a bit of drama, but it worked out in the end. We were purely being guided by what estate agents said and the letters that came through the post with Post-it notes that said, 'Read this' or 'Sign here'. We did as we were told but I am not sure any of it made a lot of sense to us. We wanted the house, so we did it.

I do not advocate this approach.

Generally, I preach education as a tool for not getting screwed. Buying a house is an area where you do not want to get screwed, so you should get educated on how the process works. To help, I'm going to give you a breakdown of a fairly typical house-buying process.

The first step is to speak to a mortgage adviser. They are responsible for finding the right mortgage for you and will help you work out your budget and what you'll need to start your application. Definitely speak to them before you start looking at houses, because your budget might turn out to be different from what you think it is. You don't want to be disappointed – or, better, low-balling yourself.

What to Look for in a Mortgage Adviser

This is a pretty weighty decision. I mean you want someone who you can trust to get you the mortgage deal that is right for you. Generally, mortgage advisers fall into two categories. There are those who are linked to a lender and will only sell you mortgages from that provider, or there are whole-market lenders who will look at all the mortgages out there and help you find the right one.

There's an obvious stronger choice here; go for the whole-market advisers – they will have access to a bigger range of deals. They may even have access to exclusive offers that you won't be able to get if you go direct or through an online broker.

Now fees are something you should think about too. There are those mortgage brokers/advisers who will charge you nothing because they get paid by the mortgage provider in the form of a commission. Others may decide to charge you a fee for their services. But which is the right one?

Honestly, I am on the fence. I don't necessarily think that a mortgage adviser who works on commission is going to be worse than one who works on a fee basis. What they do need to be is transparent; you have a right to ask how they make their money and what commission they will receive on a product. Don't be afraid to be assertive on this one. If they are being cagey about it, then maybe it is time to speak to a different broker.

How on Earth Do You Choose a House?

Choosing a house should be the fun part. In many ways it IS fun! But in others, it is bloody horrible. Firstly, NEVER look a bit above your budget. For some reason, even if you are only looking at small one-bed flats, a tiny increase in the 'maximum price' section will show you countryside mansions with swimming pools and tennis courts. Well, at least that is how it looked to us. This is a game that you cannot win. You will just feel miserable about the homes you can really afford. Looking just above what you are prepared to pay when there is a huge demand for those sorts of houses is unlikely to be fruitful.

However, there is no harm in looking for those houses that you might be able to negotiate the price down on; these could end up being within your budget. But you need to be aware of the market conditions. Lots of interest in these properties will push the price up, so do a little research or speak to an estate agent about the market before you start looking.

At this point, I am going to sound a bit like a broken record and remind you to think about what you want from a house. Remember that you don't have to go all in on a house because it is a 'great investment opportunity'. Ultimately, this is going to be your home. Think about how you are going to afford it, maintain it, live in it, and potentially work in it. First and foremost, the right house should meet the needs of your lifestyle. Both now and for as long as you plan on living in it.

My husband and I always knew that we wanted two kids. The right house therefore had to have three bedrooms and a garden that was big enough for riding a bike around. Minimum. The house we bought was pretty much at the top end of our budget at the time. Now we could afford a bigger house, but we haven't moved. Why?

Well, this house meets our needs. This house is cheap (our mortgage is affordable and bills are more than manageable), it is low-maintenance, and it is easy enough to rent out if we want to jump ship and travel the world again. It has lots of elements that suit our lifestyle. Sure, there are a few things that I would like to improve, and I am sure that when our kids get bigger we will move, but I am not going to buy the biggest house we can afford just because we can. I'll get one that suits all areas of my lifestyle, and I urge you to do the same.

At this stage, you've spoken to a mortgage adviser and you've had an offer accepted on a house. Yep? Good! Let me tell you what happens next so that you can go through the process thoroughly informed, much more than I was ten years ago.

What Else Do You Need to Know?

The next step is to sort the mortgage. You will need to be speaking to your mortgage adviser about the perfect mortgage for you. They will also ask for all the information that they need to make your application. This will include going through an affordability stress test, which will check your ability to pay your mortgage and other bills if interest rates rise in the future. It helps to have a solid plan for this and to think carefully about how much house you need.

Conveyancing is next, and probably the most nauseating part. These are your solicitors. They are the ones who deal with the legal side of things and bring all the different components together, including surveys, your mortgage and the estate agents. Finding the right conveyancer is a challenge, but one of my Instagram followers had a good tip – they found a few who were well reviewed or recommended and sent them all the same email. The one who replied first was the one that they went with.

This is an ingenious strategy because the number one beef that people have with solicitors is that they are so ridiculously slow. You should expect to be chasing them for stuff fairly regularly. Choosing a solicitor using the fastest-finger-first method seems to me like a solid system.

Not long after you've got these balls rolling, you can expect your mortgage lender to want to value the property. This is to make sure that it is worth what you are paying. This isn't normally a complicated procedure and the seller's estate agent can get involved to sort it out anyway.

What you need to know is that this ISN'T a survey.

What is a survey then? A survey is when a specialist goes and checks the house over to see if there are any issues that you are not able to see from a standard glance around. They will be able to give you a report on what they find, and estimated costs for repairs. There are different levels of surveys, so you need to pick the one that is right for the property that you are buying. Older properties, or non-standard builds, might need something more thorough. If this survey shows up anything particularly concerning, they may encourage you to have a further specialist survey completed on that particular problem.

Now while this is all going on your solicitor will be carrying out some searches for you. This will include looking at any legal technicalities on the deeds, and any environmental issues such as flooding, drainage and local authority checks. If anything shows up, they should bring it to your attention.

Slowly, it will start to come together. The searches will be completed, the survey will be done, and you'll have a mortgage offer.

A lot of paperwork will need your signature.

You'll eventually get to the stage where your solicitor says that you are ready to exchange contracts. This will also mean transferring over your deposit and signing the contracts so that you are ready to go.

Once contracts have been exchanged, it is legally binding and you can't pull out. Hello, major milestone. It is also the time when you need to get buildings and content insurance running from. Mostly because it would suck if the house burned down now and you still had to pay for it.

After this, there is a bit more legal stuff. More paperwork to sign. Oh, and your mortgage provider will release the funds. Then completion! Woo! And moving-in day!

This is the day when you can take that front door selfie for the 'gram and smile from ear to ear as you eat fish and chips on the floor of your new home. Honestly, it is the best feeling ever. My husband and I spent that evening after we moved in dreaming of all the things that we wanted to improve in our new home and all the amazing things that we would achieve while we lived there.

Unfortunately, you are not quite done with the paperwork. Thankfully, your solicitor will sort most of this. It includes paying any stamp duty and registering your ownership. They'll then sort out any money that is owed or left over, and send you any remaining paperwork. You'll likely be unpacking for a long while after this though.

I want to level with you for a moment. Buying a house is not for the faint-hearted. It is stressful. You will have to send emails and make phone calls. Ugh. You will feel the fear as you transfer over the tens of thousands of pounds that you have been saving for years. You will feel the weight of responsibility to ensure that those mortgage payments get paid.

This is why I started this chapter by urging you to think about this as the massive financial decision that it is. Let's end the passively drifting into home ownership because FOMO. You know what is coming now. Is this something you want?

Looking to the Future

At this point, I feel like most finance-y people would leave you alone and consider their job done. But the reality is that after this you still have a load more choices that you could make relating to home ownership.

You could move. Upsize or downsize. You could extend. Your friend who owns the other half might want to sell up to buy with their boyf instead. You might decide you want to quit your job and take your kids and husband around the world while you rent your house out.

So many house decisions.

The good news is that, if you've followed what I've said in this chapter up to now, then you will be in a cracking position to deal with these eventualities. Whatever you do I recommend education, reflection and conversation.

Educate yourself on your options and their implications. Reflect on whether it is the right decision and what you truly want. (I have seen so many people extend their house and then move immediately afterwards because the extension didn't fix the true problem.) Converse with all other parties involved from the start. It is literally that simple.

What I do want to talk about in more detail though is paying off your mortgage early. Should you do it?

Yes and no.

Being mortgage-free sounds amazing. You'd have complete ownership of your property and, without the mortgage payment, more money to spend every month on other more fun stuff. This is why a lot of people choose to overpay their mortgages, to clear it sooner. There are also some financial advantages to this.

By making regular overpayments on your mortgage, you will reduce the amount of interest you will pay across the duration of the mortgage term. This could work out to be worth tens of thousands, or even hundreds of thousands of pounds. Obviously, it won't feel like it at the time because it will be spread about over twenty years or something.

Also, you will be lowering your LTV or loan-to-value rate, which could save money. The more of your home that you own compared to the amount you owe on your mortgage, the better deals you are likely to be offered on your mortgage. What I mean by this is that when you come to remortgage, say at the end of a fixed deal, if you own 40 per cent you are normally offered lower interest rates than someone who owns 25 per cent.

Why wouldn't you do it then?

Mortgages are cheap. I know it doesn't feel like it when your mortgage payments eat up half your salary, but in borrowing terms they are some of the cheapest loans out there. Think about the APR on credit cards. They are normally 20–30 per cent +, whereas your mortgage interest rates are likely in the low single digits. This is cheap money.

It also goes back to the whole 'Is it a home or an investment?' argument. You could speed up the process of owning more and more of your home, until it is all yours, by overpaying. Or you could take off what you were going to overpay and invest it instead.

As I said earlier, I will give you the low-down on investing in a couple of chapters time, but for comparison let's say that you get a 7 per cent return annually on your money (on average – it goes up and down. Classic stock market!) but the interest on your mortgage is 3 per cent. Overpaying your mortgage essentially gets you a 3 per cent return on your money, but investing could get you 7 per cent. That is quite a significant difference.

There would be nothing stopping you from paying the standard mortgage payment and investing any extra cash you have, then 15 years down the line withdrawing some of your investments to pay off your mortgage.

Obviously, it is never as straightforward as that. The stock market is risky, so some people prefer the certainty of saving the interest by overpaying. People like security too, so having complete ownership of a property that you cannot be chucked out of is appealing. Emotions make this decision harder.

Hey! It is PERSONAL finances and this book is all about living life on your terms. Wanna overpay? Knock yourself out! Rather spend that money on camping equipment and spend the summer in a tent in the Scottish Highlands? If it lights you up, then it is money well spent.

I hope that by now you will realise that home ownership is no longer a linear process. There are lots of creative ways that you can fulfil your dream of owning your first home. You just need a sprinkle of creativity.

But if you've got to the end of this chapter and gone, 'NAH! I'll pass!' then good for you too. Being a homeowner is not the only thing that life is about. No one is writing, 'They lived in a massive four-bed place in the nice part of town' on your headstone, so try to keep it in perspective.

Chapter Seven

Savings, Savings, Savings!

Let's talk about saving money. First up, I want us to recognise that when we talk about saving money it can mean three things. You have saving money where you shove it in a savings account and keep it for something later on; then you have cutting back your spending; and then there's getting discounts on things that you are buying. There really should be three separate words for this, but we will have to work with what we've got.

For the next few pages, I really want to work on getting you to put more money aside in those savings accounts. On top of that, I want to make sure that your money is working its hardest for you to make even more money. Get your money to do some heavy lifting for once. You've been grafting, and so should your savings.

I am super fortunate! My parents are chronic savers. It is like their default setting for money. While the rest of the world is out there spending, my parents are hoarding cash. It's a superpower and I have been in awe of them since the day I realised it.

Saving money in this day and age though is quite a challenge.

Everything costs more and wages aren't keeping up. This means that the gap between what we earn and what we spend – which is typically the money that we would normally be saving – is smaller than ever. And it really isn't helpful when some boomer in their house that they bought in the late seventies for £200 and a biscuit tells you to cut out the Starbies and you'll be able to save too. Kindly eff off!

Because the reality is not that simple. But just because it isn't simple doesn't make it impossible. You need a different strategy, and that is what this book is all about. Making money work for you in current times.

Thankfully, there are several wonderful schemes that can help you build and grow your savings. But you need to know what you want to do with those savings first. And I don't mean whether you want a holiday or a new car. I'm talking about what the purpose is for that money that you are putting aside. You want it to fall into three broad categories: emergency fund, sinking funds and short- to medium-term goals. (I'll talk about long-term goals later.)

If you are thinking, 'Charlotte! Dearest! Why can't I just shove it all in one savings account and leave it at that?', my answer is going to be 1. Mindset and 2. Interest rates. To help you understand the thinking, here's a breakdown of each of these different categories of savings.

Emergency Funds

Without a doubt, this is the most important type of savings. Everyone needs an emergency fund. This can go by many other names too, such as a rainy-day fund and a f***-you fund. For me, this is the pot of money that takes you from panicking about money all the time to breathing free.

For me, an emergency fund is the number one contributor towards financial peace of mind.

In essence, it is a stash of cash that is kept purely for dealing with those moments when something completely unexpected has happened and you need money. Some examples include losing your job, having to take long-term sick leave or dealing with some home emergency.

I want to tell you a story that shows what I mean by 'home emergency'. A friend of mine discovered that he had a wasp nest in the walls of his house, so he called a wasp specialist to come and deal with it. Only it wasn't any old boring wasp, it was a special wasp (don't ask which one because I have forgotten) that had protection. Turns out that you can't just kick this wasp out, it needed a full rehoming service – to the tune of over £10,000. Yep! Ten grand! For wasps.

So yeah, while rare wasps living in your house is unlikely, I would like to know that if something weird like that did happen I have some money to at least cover the excess on my insurance for this sort of thing.

When it comes to preparing for things like losing your job or long-term sick leave, no one likes to think about that. But we should and we must.

As I said, an emergency fund is your peace of mind. It's that buffer so that should the worst happen you are ready for it.

How much should you have in your emergency fund then?

This is a good question and it deserves an answer. The problem is, it is quite a hotly debated topic.

What everyone agrees on is that something, literally anything, is better than nothing. If you can have a couple of hundred quid set aside then at least you won't go into debt if your car fails its MOT or your washing machine decides to give up the ghost. That sort of buffer can make a significant difference, so don't be dismissive of smaller amounts.

In an ideal world, it would be good to have a lot more than this. I'm talking thousands. Now if that made you sweat just reading it, then I understand. The thought of having thousands of pounds sitting in a bank account for 'just in case' does feel rather pointless. And even getting to that place feels like a monumental ask. I'll come back to this in a bit, okay?

But let's look at the calculation. Generally, it is agreed that you should aim for somewhere between three and six months of your outgoings. When is it three months and when should it be six? My feeling is that it depends on your circumstances. You might be able to get away with having three months if you are a fit and healthy single person with no real major responsibilities such as kids and mortgage payments. Another situation that might make it reasonable to have a lower emergency fund is if you are in a public sector job. These tend to be more stable, they normally have decent sick pay, and there are a lot of hoops for employers to jump through if they want to sack you.

If however, you are a parent, or have vulnerable adults that you look after, or you have a mortgage or lots of other financial commitments, then aim for six months. If you are self-employed, you might want to go as far as even 12 months. But I will leave you to decide whether I have stepped into ridiculous territory or not.

Remember that I am talking about expenses too. This is what you have going out every month. Not what you have coming in. What you are looking to do is to extend how long you could maintain your standard of living if you had no money coming in.

In light of this, it might be worth revisiting your budget and looking at areas where you could cut down on your spending. I love to have what I call a 'disaster budget'. This is to be whipped out in case of emergencies. It is basically a fully stripped-down budget showing all the things that I could cancel and remove at short notice and how much that would then save me a month. To do this, I went through each expense and, if it could be cancelled immediately, then it was removed from my disaster budget. This meant things like Amazon Prime would get kicked, and Netflix and Spotify. Then there were also those things like food shopping. I know I could strip that back if I needed to, so it got reduced.

This process means that, if you are willing to make some sacrifices, you can get away with having a lower amount in your emergency fund.

HOW TO STORE YOUR EMERGENCY FUND

I want to now address the issue of keeping such a large amount of money just sitting there. I am hoping that at this point you sort of understand why it is a good idea. Think back to what I said about peace of mind, okay?

But the money doesn't have to just do nothing.

One of the upsides of high inflation is that the Bank of England has sprung into action and raised interest rates. While this is fairly crappy news for borrowers, including anyone with a mortgage, it has meant some improvements in the interest rates on savings. Even if those go back down to some of the low levels we saw in 2019 and earlier, you can still look for the best interest rate you can get on these savings.

The key point to remember here is that this is your EMERGENCY fund. You need to be able to access this money at short notice. By that I mean that, if you lost your job today, you'd probably want to access at least some of that money tomorrow. Therefore, you need to be looking at instant access savings accounts. I'll talk more about these in a bit, but basically with these accounts you are probably looking at some of the crappiest rates on the market. However, there is still a big difference between the worst ones and the best ones, and it could be the difference between of a few pence of interest every year and hundreds of pounds. Put the effort in and find a good one.

Where should you look for these though?

Well, you can just do a Google search for 'best instant access savings accounts'. That'll probably take you to a website where someone has trawled through all the available accounts and will tell you the best rates. Then you can just go ahead and open that account and move your money over.

This is the simplest way to manage your emergency fund.

Now some people would argue that you are unlikely to need all of your emergency funds immediately. Obviously, this depends on whether you have £250 in there or 12 months' worth of outgoings. But assuming the latter, there is scope for spreading your emergency fund across several accounts with varying levels of access.

You could have some in an account that you can't access for six months. You'd get a higher interest rate on this, and you'd be able to keep the other half in your instant access account to use if you needed it suddenly. You'd have to be bloody sure that you could cope without that money in that timeframe though.

So yes, it is possible to stagger your emergency money across multiple accounts if you really wanted to. And yes, the extra interest on the ones without instant access would be nice. But make sure you know what you are doing and how to access each account, and offset the interest gain against the extra work required; the last thing you want to be doing when you're having to take three months off work is to spend that time firing off letters to all these banks to get your cash in a few months' time.

HOW DO YOU GET AN EMERGENCY FUND IN THE FIRST PLACE?

I want to discuss how you might go about raising the money for your emergency fund. Unfortunately, there aren't a whole load of shortcuts to take here. You are going to have to hustle a bit to build up the money. That said, I do have some advice.

Make it a goal.

Make it your focus for the next year or so to get your emergency fund built up. If you've got a side hustle, then shovel that money into your emergency fund. If you've got a tax refund, hello emergency fund. Sold some bits online, EMERGENCY FUND. Chuck everything you've got at it until you reach a level that you are happy with.

There are some caveats to this. We will discuss them more later in the book, but paying off high-interest debt is costing you money. Before you start launching every spare penny you have into your emergency fund, you might want to think about clearing some of that debt. As I said earlier though, having even a small emergency fund to deal with surprise broken kitchen appliances is always smart. Debt or no debt. It's your buffer to further debt. Many people in the industry, therefore, build a small emergency pot, then focus on debt, and then go ahead and work on their full emergency fund.

That said, you do what you love. If you think that having an emergency fund is going to bring you more peace and freedom, and you can build enough savings to cover your debt payments too, then do that. It's PERSONAL finance after all.

Sinking Funds

I love sinking funds. They're like the ultimate life hack and I swear if you can get to grips with them they will revolutionise your financial situation. Bold claim eh?! Hear me out!

Sinking funds are saving pots where you put money aside for all the different things that you will need to pay for in the future. And trust me, there are LOADS of things you could use these for.

Some people tend to overuse their emergency fund. They'll dip into it for things they know are coming up like Christmas, holidays and annual car insurance payments. That's not what your emergency fund is for. If you know the payment is coming, then you need to set up a sinking fund for it.

Back in the olden days, people would have envelopes and every month stuff some cash in there until it was needed. They might have done this to save for a new car or replace the kids' school shoes. Anything that they knew they were going to have to pay for.

This is all a sinking fund is. Except you don't need a stack of envelopes (or little tins or jam jars) to make it happen. Thankfully, the digital world has replicated these ideas and these days you can do it from most banking apps. More on that shortly.

What should you have sinking funds for then? Good ones include things such as Christmas, birthdays, any other religious or family celebrations, holidays, date nights, and anything you pay for annually, including car insurance, car tax, or your MOT, house insurance, house maintenance, car maintenance and school uniform costs. I could go on and on.

Generally, sinking funds fall into two camps: things you know are coming up and things that you pay annually. Take things that you know are coming up first. A good example of this could be a kids' birthday party. They have a birthday every year and they want a party. Why not start saving up for it now? The same goes for Christmas. You know it's coming, so get your save on.

Paying for car insurance and home insurance annually normally works out cheaper than if you opt to pay for it monthly. Therefore I like to use sinking funds for these too. Every month, I put approximately one-twelfth of the cost into a sinking fund (it's always a good idea to add a bit extra too, as things are likely to go up in cost as inflation goes up). Then when it is time to renew I pay it out of that pot. You can do this for all sorts of other payments too, such as TV licence, council tax and even your tax bill if you're self-employed.

Now I would say that there are very few true emergencies in life that would require you to dip into your actual emergency fund to pay for. My family has a house maintenance fund. This is used to redecorate the house, but also to deal with small emergencies that don't qualify as real, serious emergencies. I mean I know things are going to go wrong in my house. That's an inevitability. Consequently, I have a pot of money ready for if I need to pop down to B&Q to buy stuff for a quick repair job.

The truth is that even items like broken washing machines could be saved up for using a sinking fund. If yours is a bit on the old side, then you might want to think about setting up a sinking fund for it and chucking some money in there every month. Even if it breaks down sooner than you had hoped, the money you have in there will at least soften the blow.

Ultimately, sinking funds are a way of turning big payments into small monthly payments. It makes them more manageable and it makes the big payments less scary. Yes, it can feel as though you just have more to spend your money on each month, but you are going to have to find that money from somewhere.

Naturally, I have sinking funds for all the aforementioned stuff, such as council tax, house maintenance and my tax bills. But I really enjoy thinking up new sinking funds that I feel would improve my financial situation. One that I recently added was a 'school stuff' fund. Every month, I stick a tenner into this pot, and then I use it for all the random requests that my kids bring home from school. This can be anything from a school trip to a bag of sugar or Christmas jumper day or wear something yellow day. Most months I don't need £10 for stuff, but in other months (November and December, I'm looking at you) I need £40.

I like to have sinking funds for fun stuff too. Like, I have one for books. Again, a few pounds a month goes in there and then, if there's a book I want, I've got the money. There's another for paddleboard stuff that covers my waterway licence each year and then purchasing any new accessories or gear that takes my fancy.

Of course, these more fun ones are completely optional, but I like to spread the cost of my fun as much as I spread of the cost of the mundane and the boring. It just makes sense to me.

LET'S TALK ABOUT ONLINE SINKING FUNDS

Earlier I mentioned that your nan would have sinking funds in envelopes, but now we get to enjoy the digital equivalents. Time to talk about what I mean by this.

Most high street banks will allow you to open as many basic savings accounts as you like, and these days most of them allow you to name the account whatever you like too. Therefore, you could have a dozen savings accounts open, all labelled things like 'Christmas and birthdays', 'Car tax' and 'TV licence.' But the newer digital banks are offering a slightly better solution than this.

Starling, Monzo and Chase all burst onto the banking scene and turned it on its head. They offered features and a new level of convenience that we didn't know we needed. One of these features is pots or spaces (they have different names depending on the bank you are with, but technically they're the same thing.)

Rather than requiring you to open several separate bank accounts, these banks allow you to create subsections within your main account. You can just section off your money. No individual account numbers, no setting up direct debits to move your money, no multiple savings account applications. Just a designated space within your existing account. Personally, I think it is bloody genius.

I utilise these every month, and have automated payments set up to move my money directly into these accounts on payday. I also have a round-up feature turned on that means whenever I spend money from the main account it rounds up the cost and moves the difference into one of these pots. Plus, banks are adding more and more functionality to these spaces all the time. Starling now allows you to have a virtual bank card for each of your spaces, so you can spend directly from that pot. In theory, you could set up your car insurance to come directly out of that sinking fund.

The future is now!

Short- To Medium-Term Goals

After you've dealt with saving for your emergency fund and you've got your sinking funds all set up and have money flying into those every month, then you can look at the real fun stuff – savings for your short- to medium-term goals. Yep! I managed to make that sound supremely boring.

But these are the fun savings. This is saving for a new car, a family holiday, a new house, that kitchen extension or the new TV you've had your eye on. It is about achieving those dreams you've had in your mind all this time.

For these savings, you can set any amount you want or that suits your budget. The more you save the faster you will achieve your goal. And that in itself is super motivational.

If you have a deadline for these savings, then you can use this super-simple formula to help you work out how much you need to save:

Amount needed (divided by) number of months = amount to save per month

Personally, I recommend that you create some sort of automation to move this money across. You want to treat it like another bill that you have to pay and move it over into your savings account as soon as the money hits your account. Then you won't miss it.

But I wouldn't stop there either. You may well be in the habit of saving now, particularly if you slogged your butt off to build your emergency fund, and, after all that creativity, you'll might be good at making more money to chuck into your savings pot. So do this too.

If you have a side hustle or you get some Christmas money, you can send that straight in the direction of your savings. What you normally see when people are working towards a big goal like this is that their progress towards that goal picks up massively towards the end. It is slow and steady at the beginning, but as they see the goal in sight suddenly the whole thing accelerates.

Back in Chapter Two, you learned all about how to figure out what you actually want and how to motivate yourself to stick to these goals. You need those skills now more than ever and, if you can get to grips with what you REALLY want from your life, it will make saving this money even easier.

It is all about harnessing the motivational power that comes from knowing what you want. Use that to avoid all that temptation and speed that money into your savings account.

Let's talk about that savings account then. Where are you going to keep all this money?

WHERE TO SAVE FOR SHORT- TO MEDIUM-TERM GOALS

Firstly, I want to address why I haven't included long-term goals in this section. Well, I personally believe that savings accounts aren't where you want to be keeping any money that you don't need in the next five years. That's what investing is for and there's a whole chapter on that coming up.

However, short- and medium-term goals don't want to be subject to the volatility of the stock market, so you need to be keeping those in low-risk accounts, and a savings account is perfect for this.

Looking at short-term goals, these are things that you want the money for in two years or less. Chances are you want to keep this money in some sort of easy access account, because you'll want to be able to get it out fairly quickly. But you could choose an account that requires a few days' notice or has a limited number of withdrawals per year. This might get you a better interest rate, and the restrictions on accessing your money might stop you from dipping into it regularly.

REGULAR SAVINGS ACCOUNTS

Another great alternative here is a regular saver account. These are aimed at people who are looking to save money regularly, and they typically offer a bonus interest rate if you can save a consistent amount over the year. What happens normally is that you will choose an amount within that bank's limits to save, and then you save that amount every month. Then at the end of the year you'll get paid a nice lump sum of interest and be able to withdraw all your money. But, if you don't pay in, or you take some money out, you could lose all or some of the bonus interest. This makes them a fantastic tool to not only boost your savings but keep you motivated to keep saving.

There are lots of these accounts around but they all have different terms and conditions, so you will have to look at the rules for each. They may for example have a range of minimums and maximums that you can pay in each month. Or they might require you to hold a current account with their bank first. Or they might offer this service for one year or two years. Or they might have different penalties for withdrawing your money. But I am certain that there will be one out there that is right for you.

FIXED-TERM ACCOUNTS

Another option if you are looking to save for the more medium term, so anywhere between about two and ten years, is to look at locking some of your money away in a fixed-term account and enjoying the increased interest rates that come with this.

The way these work is that you agree to put some of your savings into a savings account for one, two, three, five or even ten years, and not touch it. In return for doing this, the bank will thank you by paying you a higher interest rate. Naturally, the longer you agree to leave it in there, the better the interest rate. That said, you have to be pretty sure that you are happy to leave that money untouched for the duration. So this works well for people who already have a good chunk of money in their emergency fund and in an easy-access savings account.

If there is some sort of weird change in your life circumstances and you do need to access that money, you typically still can, but at a cost. You will be required to request a withdrawal of your money, which could take a few days or even as long as a few weeks. You'll lose at least some of the interest benefits and there may even be a fee to pay. So, like I said, you need to be sure that you want to take out the money.

The key to all of this is getting your money to work as hard as it can for you by getting the best interest rates. Don't let your money just sit there in some lousy account that is paying practically nothing for the privilege. Opening a new savings account is super easy and you can do it online at a time that is convenient for you. This is not something to be lazy about. A quick Google search will show you the best savings accounts out of all the wide variety of options so you can choose which one is right for you. Open it in a few minutes and potentially make hundreds, or possibly thousands, in interest.

And check these regularly too. The best account for you now might not be the best one in six months. Banks and building societies are constantly trying to outdo each other and get new customers. Look out for better accounts every few months, and swap about if you have to. This is not an age when loyalty is rewarded. Change your savings account as often as you change your socks if you want. Don't leave money on the table.

ISAS

I couldn't write a chapter on savings and not mention the glorious ISA. ISA stands for Individual Savings Account and it is a tax-free wrapper that goes around a savings or investment account that means that whatever you save or invest is free from any tax. So yeah, you wanna know about these.

There are four main types of ISA. I'll speak more about leveraging ISAs for investments in Chapter Ten, but for now I wanted to give you a brief overview of all four and how they can be used to accelerate your savings and help you reach your goals.

Before you learn all the ins and outs of each one, I

want to tell you the rules that govern all of the ISAs. Firstly, all UK residents over the age of eighteen can open an ISA, and there are also versions for children. You are currently allowed to pay in a maximum of £20,000 across all types of ISA in each financial year, which runs from 6 April to 5 April the following year. You are only allowed to pay into one of each type of ISA in a tax year.[16]

You won't pay any tax. This includes interest on your cash (in a cash ISA) and dividend tax or capital gains tax on investments (in a stocks and shares ISA). This can be highly beneficial as your money grows, as you'll earn more and more interest, or your investments will appreciate.

Quick Note

It is worth mentioning here that there are a couple of other circumstances where you may not have to pay tax on your savings. The first is by utilising the starting rate for savings, which leans into your income tax personal allowance. Let me try to explain.

Currently, you can earn £12,570 without paying any income tax. If what you earn from your job, side hustles, rental properties and whatnot is less than that, then you won't have to pay income tax. Now your savings interest is also on that list. But it does go a bit further than this. The government has agreed to add £5,000 to that personal allowance figure, so, if all your income is less than £17,570, then you won't have to pay tax on YOUR INTEREST FROM SAVINGS. Now I'm shouting that bit because you may still have to pay tax on your other income, like from your job.[17]

You could also be entitled to use the personal savings allowance, which allows some people to earn £1,000 in interest on their savings in any account in a financial year and not pay tax on it. But there are some restrictions on this. Your personal savings allowance amount is linked to your income tax bracket and your earnings. Therefore, if you are a basic-rate payer or less, then you get the full £1,000. Higher-rate payers get £500 and additional-rate payers get nothing.

The bottom line is you might not NEED an ISA to benefit from tax-free savings, but honestly, they are the easiest to ensure that you aren't paying any and they're free, so I'm a bit like, 'Why not?' Now let's look at the different types like I promised.

Cash ISA

This is the one that 100 per cent deserves to be in this chapter, because it is essentially a savings account. You stick your money in there and you earn interest. Then that interest is guaranteed to be tax-free. There's nothing complicated about these really. But they do vary between banks, so I recommend that you do your research.

Some variations that you might see include different interest rates, and this is important, so make sure that you shop around to get the best one. Remember: no laziness when it comes to interest rates. There might also be restrictions on withdrawals, so you may be able to withdraw your money any time you like, or you may only be able to take it out a few times a year. The other thing to consider is flexibility. Some, called flexible ISAs, will allow you to take your money out and put it back in without it further eating into your ISA limit, and some won't.

So what I mean by this is that let's say you pay £20,000 into your ISA on 6 April (lucky you!) but then in May you decide you want to take £5,000 out for a holibobs. Now a flexible ISA will say that you can pay that £5,000 back in at some point later in the financial year. However, a 'normal' ISA will say, 'Nah mate! You paid in your £20k, I don't care that you've taken a bit out. You're done for this year!' Does that make sense? Good!

Stocks and shares (S&S) ISA

Next up is the investment ISA, which I will talk about in a lot more detail in Chapter Ten because this ISA is soooo useful when it comes to investing. But in essence, it acts as a tax-free container for whatever you want to invest in.

The usual rules for ISAs apply, and you can get flexible versions of these too. Who you open your ISA with will determine what you can invest in, but there is a huge range of providers, so there is bound to be one that suits your investing needs.

Tax-wise, your investments outside of an ISA are normally subject to both dividend tax and capital gains tax. Dividend tax is a tax on the money paid to you by a company out of their profits, and capital gains tax is a tax on the money made from the increasing value of an item. Both come with their own tax-free allowances. But in an S&S ISA you don't have to worry about either of these.

Lifetime ISA (LISA)

In Chapter Six, I talked about how useful these ISAs are for people who are looking to buy their first home. But there are a few varieties of LISA and a few different rules depending on the one you choose, so I want to make sure that you understand them before you dive head first into signing up for one.[18]

Here are the different rules:

- You must be aged between 18 and 40 to sign up for these, but you can continue to pay into them until you are 50.
- You can only pay in a maximum of £4,000 a year, and this is part of the total £20k limit across all ISAs. So if you use the £4k in your LISA, then that leaves you able to pay in £16k to the others.
- The government gives you a 25 per cent bonus on whatever you pay in up to £1,000 a year. Win!

As well as these additional rules, though, there are some additional perks. Therefore, you might want to think about using them to help you achieve your goals. But again, wait – you can only use an ISA for two things.

The first is to save for your FIRST home, and there are rules on this too, so go back to Chapter Six if you've forgotten what they are. The other is to save for retirement. Whatever you are planning on doing with that money (first home or retirement), you have to follow the rules above. But you can choose to sign up for either a cash version or a S&S version. Typically, those working on saving for their first home would choose a cash LISA and those saving for retirement would go for the investment version, but honestly it is up to you. But why? Well, the reason for this is based on the length of time you spend saving into these accounts. When buying a house, you might save for five to ten years, which if you went for the investment version could mean that your money loses value at the exact moment you need it. That length of time is generally considered too short to ride the ups and downs of the stock market and come out on top. Conversely, choosing the cash option for retirement means that you could miss out on the long-term growth you can often expect from investments. You want your money to work harder for your retirement, because you have more time.

Innovative finance ISA

These are the most obscure ISAs and there are only 17,000 people in the UK who actually have one.[19] And to be fair, I get it. They are designed for people who want to invest in peer-to-peer loans and buy companies' debts. They might be for you if you have lots of money and want to try a different type of investing with the tax-free benefits. Or they might be for you if you are a massive finance nerd. It's not something normal people like you and me are that interested in. But at least for now you know they exist and that they follow the general ISA rules.

Help to Save

So far in this chapter, you might be feeling like I have assumed that you have money to save. In a way I have, because I believe that you will get there. Once you have finished this book, you'll have all the tools to make saving money happen for you in this modern world. But, additionally, I don't want you to feel like you are being overlooked if you don't have a huge amount of money to save right now.

This is why I want to tell you about the government's Help to Save scheme. This is one of the brilliant tools that exist in today's world to help people who are struggling to save to get ahead. And you have to take advantage of anything that is on offer these days.

Help to Save is a savings scheme that helps certain people who receive working tax credit or universal credit to get help building up a pot of savings. You can pay between £1 and £50 into this account in any calendar month for up to four years. The 'help' part comes in because the government tops this up by a bonus 50p for every £1 that you save.

This means that you could save £50 a month and get

an extra £25 from the government. Bonuses are paid out at the end of the second and fourth years, and if you close the account early you will miss out on the next bonus. You can withdraw the money if you need to, but again you will miss out on the bonus on this money.

The financial world that we are living in is a lot different from what it was even ten to fifteen years ago, so it makes absolute sense to get your savings working with the systems and schemes that are on offer. You are definitely NOT going to be shoving that money under your mattress like your grandad did. And I forbid you to leave money sitting in your current account earning naff-all interest when there are accounts out there that will make you so much more. Please, let's learn to make our savings thrive!

Automation

Before I wrap this chapter up, I want to re-emphasise a point I made willy-nillily about automating your savings. This is a total life hack and I don't want you to pass it up.

I have rattled on about how I don't want you to be lazy when it comes to getting the best interest rates on your savings. But once you have done that, then I am 100 per cent here for the laziness, and the way that you can harness that laziness is by automating your savings. This is the real perk of living in this time; technology is capable of doing so much for us, and when it comes to money I WANT it to do it for me, because I am not entirely sure that I trust myself to do it, if I am honest.

Automation can be used for all areas of your finances. You likely already have direct debits set up to pay for your bills and rent. (If you don't, you can get on that too).

So I touched on automation when I spoke about sinking funds and how I have a regular payment that moves money from my main account into my little savings pots as soon as I get paid. This means that these pots grow without me needing to do anything. Plus, because that money disappears before I get time to get my spendy mitts on it, I forget that it is there.

I also mentioned automation when it comes to those short- and medium-term goals. I told you to set up a regular amount each month and get that to come out on payday too. Again, you'll be working on those goals without having to lift a finger and you can just sit back and watch that pot grow.

Fintech has come a long way, though, and it can do a lot more than just move money from your current account to your savings account on payday. For example, like I have said before, you could use round-ups to boost your savings. This means that if you spend £4.50 on coffee from your current account, it will round up that spend to £5 and put the extra 50p in your savings account. Now I'm betting that you pretty much chalked that coffee up as being a fiver in your head anyway, so you are missing nothing. Some banks and apps will allow you to boost this too. I have a 5x multiplier on my round-ups. This means that it rounds up my spending, times it by five and shoves that amount into my savings. Accelerated money moves!

One app has a fun feature that moves an amount you set into your 'rainy-day fund' every time it rains in your area, which I think is just adorably fun. I have also heard of apps in other countries that will move money into your savings every time you hit snooze on your phone. I need this feature in my life NOW!

Technology has always been the greatest benefit of our generation, and now we can use it to give us a leg-up with our savings and I am here for it!

Chapter Eight

Dealing with Debt

The variety of debt available is more vast and complicated than ever. Your nan might have had a mortgage and a loan from the bank, but you've got those plus car finance, six credit cards that you juggle for different 0 per cent deals and a Klarna account for an outfit that you bought for your cousin's second wedding. Managing this debt is a part-time job in itself and, with rising costs and stagnant wages, there seems to be no escape.

The average personal unsecured debt in the UK has recently reached a new high of £4,087.[20] This means that there are some people who are lucky enough to have less than this and some who unfortunately have more. But the key message is that as a society we now have more debt, and, with a cost of living crisis and rising demands on our money, debt is becoming harder and harder to manage.

The good news is that you can get debt-free. And stay there.

My first experience with the concept of debt came as a child. The family TV had broken so naturally I was devastated and agreed to assist my mum in purchasing a new one. I was also a bit of a tech nerd and was positively ecstatic at the thought of getting to pick out a new one. Anyway, after a good mooch around Dixons in the high street, my mum found the one. A bloody massive CRT (those old TVs with the massive bit at the back) and it came in silver. Phwoar!

At the till, the bloke asked my mum if she wanted to do buy it now and pay in six months with no fees for paying in six months' time. I was like, 'What is this magic?' My mum agreed and I stood patiently as she handed over all her details and the man drew up the credit agreement. What my poor mum didn't know at the time was that she was about to get assaulted with questions on the journey home.

'What is a credit agreement? Does this mean you haven't paid? Why didn't you just pay now? Why did he need to know where we live? Do we not have enough money for a TV?'

Thankfully, my mum is used to me and just rolled her eyes, sighed deeply and proceeded to answer my questions truthfully. She explained that it was possible to borrow the money to buy some things and this could be a good way for people to buy stuff they can't afford right now. She then explained that if you do this with things that you don't NEED, though, it can get tricky. She continued that she did have the money, but because it didn't cost any more to pay later she was going to leave that money in her bank account and earn some interest for the next six months.

I thought my mum was well smart!

This was a great first introduction to debt. It taught me that it existed and that it could be good, but also that it could spell trouble if not used correctly. And my mum and dad continued to encourage me to save up for the things that I wanted rather than looking at borrowing money instead.

When I was older, my parents got their first credit card. They were so sensible with it. They would buy groceries and petrol on it and pay it off every month. Like clockwork. I sort of didn't understand why. I'm still not sure I do, as they don't get any perks on their credit card, but, trust me, I've had words about that.

When I turned eighteen, I got a phone contract and learned all about my financial responsibilities and quietly enjoyed the fact that I was building myself a credit score while mostly using it to play songs and message my mates to ask when they were coming round for pre-drinks.

As a result of my parents' cautious approach to finance, I learned to steer clear of debt from a young age and have enjoyed a relatively debt-free adulthood. But it hasn't been completely avoidable. It is practically impossible to do that these days. Yes, I have a mobile phone that is half paying for the handset and half paying for the service. I have a credit card, but I pay that off every month. I had an overdraft at uni that made my parents flip their lids when they found out how much I owed. And I have had a personal loan to buy a car.

Thankfully though, my debt has always been manageable.

But this isn't true for everyone. I hope that, as we navigate this chapter, you will learn how to make your debt more manageable for you, and even develop the tools to clear it completely if you want to.

What Is Debt?

A good starting point is to get a good definition of what debt is, and who better to consult than the *Oxford English Dictionary*:

'That which is owed or due; anything (as money, goods, or service) which one person is under obligation... A sum of money or a material thing.'[21]

Basically, it is money that has been borrowed and that you have to pay back in some way. In most instances, this is via some formal arrangement with a bank, credit provider or some other financing service.

You can break debt down into two main categories: secured and unsecured. Secured debt is that which is linked to a product. The most common type of secured debt would be a mortgage: debt that is linked to a home. What this means is that, if you cannot pay, then your mortgage provider could kick you out, sell your house and recover their money. Car finance is another example. You stop paying, they'll come get your car back.

Unsecured debt is anything that is not linked to one particular product. This includes credit card debt, personal loans and overdrafts. This is more about general borrowing to cover smaller costs. It is much riskier for the lenders and this is why it normally comes with much higher interest rates.

Think about mortgages. They have interest rates that are some of the lowest on the market for debt because the banks know that they can get their money back if you can't pay. Whereas how can they get their money back for that brunch you paid for on your credit card? That's going to be hard to recover, so the rates on your credit card are higher; potentially A LOT higher – likely to be in the teens and upwards.

It is worth mentioning here that these types of debt are just the more formal arrangements; it could be that you have borrowed money from family and friends. This is debt too and, while they may not be charging you interest on it, you likely feel a sense of responsibility to pay them back.

Is There Such a Thing as Good Debt and Bad Debt?

Lots of people like to think that some debt is good and some debt is bad, and they could be right. However, your view on this is likely going to come from an accumulation of your experiences and emotions around debt in the past.

Debt that has led to struggle, poorly managed finance or ill-feeling between family members is going to feel like it is bad. This is completely valid and probably the way debt feels more often than not.

But many would argue that mortgages are a form of

good debt. Or they are at least more socially acceptable. This is largely because they enable people to buy an appreciating asset. In normal-people speak, this means something that is going to make them money in the long run. People who are particularly financially confident will take this a step further and borrow more money for the purposes of investing it to see a return on that money. A good example of this is buying rental property.

When asked, most people would probably identify credit cards as bad debt. They can be a slippery slope for people who are spending more than they earn, and can get you into financial holes that are hard to get out of.

Conversely, credit cards can be used as a money-making tool, and are by many people. Myself included. Hell, thanks to my credit card I will be getting £400 in cashback next month, and all I did was buy stuff that I was going to buy anyway and then pay it back every month.

In short, debt isn't inherently bad.

However, with poor education, slow wage growth and a struggling economy, more and more people are turning to debt as a solution to their shortfalls in income. But this creates further challenges and uncertainty down the line. Debt sold as a solution to people's financial problems is bad. And as a society, we need to recognise the role that these credit providers play in perpetuating financial insecurity in many households.

Should You Pay Off Your Debt Then?

Rather than answer this question for you, I want to instead get you to think about what a life without debt would look like for you. A good starting point would be to think about how much you are spending each month on paying off that debt. Do those debt payments make budgeting hard for you and your family? What other things are you going without because you have to pay off that debt each month? What would you do with the spare cash if you weren't using it to pay for stuff you bought in the past?

Yes, yes! I know that some of these are slightly leading questions and as a mathematician I should know better. But I do believe that you could achieve a much higher level of financial freedom if you didn't have debt.

Think about it.

If you had no debt, no mortgage and only a few bills to pay, you could decide maybe to take a few months off work and live off a small savings pot for a bit. This could be to have children, to travel, to work on a side hustle, or to just sit in the garden sipping cocktails and ploughing through your 'to be read' list.

Or maybe you could start saving to buy your first home. Or your second home. Or maybe you could look at investment options for that money. That could start a string of financial decisions that lead to you retiring early and living your best life sitting on a balcony in Italy in your fifties.

The fewer financial obligations you have, the more freedom you have. That's the bottom line.

And with debt being one of the biggest financial obligations many of us have, perhaps it is time to consider shifting it. Once and for all!

HOW TO PAY IT OFF

At this point, I am going to assume that you do have some debt and that I have convinced you that it might be a good idea to get rid of it. Yes? Good!

This is the point where I am going to tell you some strategies for making this happen. I am a person who likes to have options (see above) and therefore I think that, when it comes to paying off debt, you should have a series of strategies to choose from so that you can find the perfect one to fit your lifestyle and current circumstances.

Underlying each of the four methods that I am going to tell you about, though, should be you regularly sending money towards your debts with the aim of paying them off sooner. You can treat this in the same way as you did your savings in Chapter Seven: set up a monthly direct debit and then, whatever spare cash you have, chuck it towards your debt and watch it gradually disappear over time.

So let's look at the four systems that you can use:

1. Debt Snowball

   This method was popularised by American financial 'guru' Dave Ramsey and, even though he really ain't my cup of tea, it has proven highly successful for a lot of people who are looking to get out of debt.

The starting point with this, and all the methods really, is to write down all your debts. You need to know how much you owe, the minimum payment for each and the interest rate. Then you are going to list them in order of how much you owe, smallest to largest debt.

This becomes the order in which you are going to focus on paying off these debts. You make the minimum payments on each of them, and all that extra money you have assigned to paying off debt goes on that smallest balance first.

The thought process behind this one is that because this first debt is your smallest you will clear it much more quickly, get a kick out of clearing it and feel so good that it will motivate you to work on the next one. Obviously, that will be a little bit more challenging as it will take longer, but you will be riding on the high of clearing that first one.

Now, for that second debt you can add the minimum payment you're putting towards the first debt to your total each month and send that towards the second debt too. You are still paying all those minimum payments on the others, but as that first one is gone you can use that spare cash and put it towards the next one. It's the snowball effect. Hence the name.

You continue to do this with each of your debts and, as you clear each one, you have more money to put towards the next one each month. It can be a long process, but you will find that, as time passes and you pay off more and more of your debts, you'll see the endpoint accelerating towards you.

2. Debt Avalanche
   The general idea behind this one is the same as with the snowball, but rather than looking at your smallest balance first you aim for the one with the highest interest rate. This is your most expensive debt, so from a financial point of view it makes sense to get rid of it first.

   Once you have the full list of your debts, you need to list them in the order highest interest rate to lowest interest rate. This is the order in which you will need to tackle them. Again, you pay the minimum payments on all and use any additional funds to work on clearing that first debt.

   Then as you clear them you use that money to work on the next one, and so on and so forth until you clear them all. The main advantage of this method is that it works out the cheapest; the expensive debt goes first and leaves you working towards the cheapest debts.

3. Largest Minimum Payment First
   Unfortunately, this one doesn't have a cute snow-related name. Perhaps I should come up with one?

   It starts the same as the other two: make a list of all those debts, including the cost of the minimum payments. This time I want you to write them in the order largest minimum payment to smallest. And the focus here is on clearing the debts that take the most out of your monthly budget first.

   The reasoning here is that, when you clear the debts with the highest minimum payments first, you create more room in your budget. You can then use this money to help with paying off the next one, and you are going to see a huge difference in how quickly you pay off the next one because you will have a huge extra chunk of cash to chuck at it.

Plus, even if something in your life changes before you can finish paying off all your debts, you are still going to be grateful that you cleared those which took the most money out of your budget first. It will automatically give you a lot more freedom.

4. You Make Me Angry

I think this is my favourite one. This one very much leans into your emotions and leverages that to get you to pay off your debts as quickly as possible. If, for example, you have some debt that you took out for an ex and they never paid you back, I would bet that you are very angry about that. Or perhaps you have a credit card balance that you built up when you were young and stupid. I bet that doesn't exactly light you up either. Now take that anger and use it to help you stay focused on paying off your debts.

Just like the other three methods, you are going to write out all your debts – but this time put the one that makes you angriest at the top and get super motivated at paying that off first. By leaning on the emotion you have towards this debt, you will likely find that you throw everything you have at it just to see it gone.

This is an awesome way to get the ball rolling on your debt pay-off journey.

Once you have this one out of the way, you can work

on the others from the list above however you like. You will feel so much better with the 'You Make Me Angry' debt out of the way and it will inspire you to continue on the path to debt freedom.

Whatever strategy you choose to use to take you to a debt-free life, I want you to track it and celebrate the milestones. Use a tracker that you colour in and stick on your fridge, share your journey on social media and allow yourself a treat when you hit a big milestone. It is all part of keeping motivated and on this journey for the long haul. No one can do it on their own and in silence. If you need to tell someone, then you can always send me a message on Instagram or ping me an email.

Credit Scores

I can't talk about debt without talking about credit scores, and yet they seem almost in conflict with each other. I've just spent multiple pages telling you to sack off the debt and yet you and I both know that having a good credit score is a powerful thing.

What is a credit score then? Well, it is a rough guide to your creditworthiness. Again with the fancy words, but it basically means if someone lends you money how well can you be trusted to pay that money back? The higher the score, the more you can be trusted. They aren't the complete picture though. In order to get a full understanding, you would need to look at your entire credit report, which is what most lenders would do before giving you their money. Your credit score is just a rough guide to what is in the report.

But the thing is, to get a credit score you have to have had some sort of experience with borrowing money and paying it back. You read that right: you need a good score to get the money, but you can't get a good score without having the money in the first place. It's the ultimate catch-22.

Thankfully, some good money habits when you are young can go a long way towards helping you build a good score without having to borrow any money. Things like getting on the electoral roll and having your name on certain bills can contribute to building this picture of you as someone who makes payments on time every time, and that's what they want to see.

Given that I've told you to sack off the debt, though, what's the point in even trying? Well, a good credit score could be useful if you want to get a mortgage, or even if you want to rent a house, and sometimes employers even do credit checks on potential employees. The relevance of credit scores is seeping out into more and more areas of our lives.

If your score is a bit low, what can you do then? Well, the best thing to do is access your full credit report and discover what is contained within it. This will help you highlight the areas that you need to work on.

There are three main credit reference agencies (CRAs) in the UK: Experian, Equifax and TransUnion. They will hold information about your previous dealing with credit, but there might be some discrepancies between the three.

I recommend that you request your report from all of them. All CRAs allow you to check your credit score for free and offer a free trial that allows you to access your credit report.

Once you have access to this information you can identify areas that you may need to work on. It could be that you need more exposure to debt; using a credit card carefully could help with this. Alternatively, your credit utilisation may be too high, which means that you are using too much of the debt that is available to you aka you've over-borrowed and you may need to pay some of that off.

There are lots of things that can affect your credit score and, if this is something that is important to you, then it is worth putting in the time to improve it. I know many people who have decided to work on their credit scores and have seen significant improvements in just a short period.

Buy Now Pay Later

One of the newest and frankly most worrying forms of debt comes via a little app that allows us to spread the cost of even small items over three, four or five payments. And that little app isn't just one app, it is many apps and is now pretty much embedded in our shopping experience.

I am talking about the likes of Klarna and Clearpay, which encourage us to spread the cost of our clothes shopping, beauty products, hotel stays, and now even groceries, over several smaller payments. But it is not just these companies that are offering these services. PayPal offers them too, as do Amazon, and many banks now have their own service. It is everywhere.

What's wrong with it though? This is a good question. On the surface of things, it seems like Buy Now Pay Later could be a useful tool for helping people to manage their spending. Plus, it allows them to reduce these expenses into smaller and consequently more manageable payments. This should in theory be quite helpful. Instead, it tends to have the opposite effect and encourage people to spend money that they don't have.

The ease of signing up for these systems, which are embedded into the payments functions of most shops, means that there are some cases of people signing up and not really knowing what they have signed up for. It is important to remember that this is still debt. You are borrowing money.

On top of this, if you miss a payment or you can't pay they will report it to the credit reference agencies, and it could have an impact on your credit score. Imagine if you couldn't get a mortgage because you forgot to make a payment on a dress you bought for your mate's hen do ten years ago. You'd kick yourself.

What is even more frustrating is that these services have appeared on the market around the same time as we all have less cash. Your wages have fallen in real terms over the last few years and suddenly there is a product that can apparently help you afford the same stuff you were affording before. Yeah, it doesn't sound quite right, does it?

My advice is to avoid using these services at all. If you can't afford that dress in full now, then you probably shouldn't be spreading it over three months either. Sorry if that ain't what you want to hear, but I swear I have your best interests at heart. Trust!

Debt as a Force for Good

I want you to imagine a time three to five years from now when you are debt-free, you've got money in your emergency fund and you feel pretty secure with your financial situation. Those bills are getting paid and you are enjoying the fun things in life too. Perhaps then you start thinking about how you can level up your finances even further.

At this point, you might start looking at rewards and cashback credit cards. And it wouldn't be a terrible idea.

That said, I do want to stick in a caveat before I go any further. If you have had your butt hurt by debt, maybe just don't go near it again. If you found yourself in such a pickle that you didn't know where to turn and needed help from a debt help charity, then maybe just relish this new happy place that you are in. You don't need this level-up. I've got more coming for you anyway.

With that out there I want to talk about using those credit cards. Earlier on in this chapter, I said I had one, and I would be lying if I told you that I didn't make a good amount of cashback from it. And cashback isn't the only thing you can get. Some people use them for airmiles and travel around the world for free.

They take discipline though.

I mean bloody hell, if I don't keep myself in check I can watch that credit card bill go up and up each month. Knowing that I have that card means I know I can buy most things that I want. But I shouldn't because I can't afford them. And I do have to pay for them eventually.

If you are new on this journey, then a good starting point is to pick one thing that you pay for regularly and use your credit card to pay for that and only that. I first started using mine to buy petrol. I was paying for it a couple of times a month and it wasn't my biggest expense. Plus, I got a sense of control from knowing in advance what it would cost me.

Over time I added groceries to that as they were a significant monthly expense but also a necessary one. This meant that I was still staying within budget, but could capitalise on the cashback benefits.

Every month I receive a bill and, this is the important part, I PAY IT OFF IN FULL.

I think I have had that credit card for 12 years now, and I haven't ever carried a balance on it. And nor would I want to, because the interest rate on that card is bloody extortionate. I have a direct debit set up on it and it gets paid off in full when I get paid. I keep it simple and I reap the benefits.

Debt can be damaging to your finances and consequently to your well-being. But you can exist within the systems that support debt, and benefit from them. These credit card bonuses are a good example of that, but they aren't for the faint of heart. You need a high level of financial control and resilience.

If it's not for you, then I fully support that. I have lots of other ways that you can earn cashback and boost your finances. Focus on paying off that debt and staying well away from it because, I promise you, your life will be richer for it.

Chapter Nine

So You've Got a Pension. Now What?

I bloody love a pension!

Any time I hear anyone talking about pensions, I want in on that conversation, because they are so rarely talked about. The nerd in me has always found this strange because pretty much everyone these days has one, but yet we treat them like a dirty secret that should never be spoken about in public. But it's money. Your money. And normally quite a lot of it too.

I spent fourteen years as a teacher and as a result have a pension via the Teachers' Pension Scheme, which is widely regarded as one of the best ones out there. I'm very lucky, I know, but I did have to teach teenagers maths for all those years to earn it. Let me tell you that that AGED me. I deserve that pension, okay? But disappointingly, the pension I've got now isn't as good as the one I got when I signed up to the profession.

Pensions are basically seeing a gradual decline in quality. My parents have a few pensions from their various jobs, and I would take a guess that most of them are better than what is being offered to employees now.

My teacher's pension started off as a final salary pension but, after a couple of years in the industry, there was a shake-up and they moved to a career average model. I'm not going to bore you with the details, but essentially I now pay more and will get less pension as a result. It sucks.

More workplaces are looking to cut costs by reducing the amount of money they contribute to their employees' pensions. Many have switched from a more secure style to riskier models to reduce their own liability on the pension front.

What I am trying to say is that our pensions aren't looking as good as those of our parents. You will live longer, things cost more and your pension is crappier. Great... This is why pension education is absolutely crucial, because you don't have to roll over and accept this. There are actions that you can take to keep your pension healthy and on track to support the sort of lifestyle you are hoping to live in your non-working years.

But I feel like I need to cover some basics before I get too deep into this.

What Is a Pension?

Legal and General describe it as 'a tax-efficient way to save for retirement'[22] and I quite like that description. It requires you to make regular payments into it over the course of your working life, with the view that once you reach a certain age you can either reduce the amount you work or stop working entirely and live off the money that you have been putting into your pension.

There are a few different options though, and not all pensions are created equally. But they do all ultimately aim to serve the same purpose, which is to provide retirement income. This can happen in a variety of ways.

DEFINED CONTRIBUTION PENSIONS

Let's talk about Defined Contribution Pensions (DC pensions) first. These are the most common type of pension and are essentially a form of investment account. You pay money into an investment pot and it is invested either under your direction or on your behalf, with the idea being that the money will make more money and you can live off that later.

With this type of pension, you are naturally at risk of the fluctuations of the stock market. Your money can go down as well as up. Some people have come unstuck because the value of their pension has dropped right at the point when they wanted to retire, forcing them to work longer or have a reduced standard of living in their later years.

Defined contribution pensions are more commonly offered by businesses that operate in the private sector, but they are available to normal people who want to pay into a personal pension in addition to or instead of their work pension.

There are a couple of ways that you can access this money at the point where you finally say, 'Eff this, I'm retiring!' You could just make regular withdrawals from the pot and live off that, known as drawdown, or you could exchange all or part of the money for an annuity, which will provide a monthly payment for life. Alternatively, you can just take the cash and run. The choice you make will depend on your personal circumstances and likely the tax implications, because you will probably have to pay tax on it too.

DEFINED BENEFIT PENSIONS

These are pretty much considered the holy grail of pensions (the Teachers' Pension Scheme is a type of DB pension). The NHS offers a type of DB pension too, along with many other businesses in the public sector. They used to be found in the private sector as well, but were either poorly managed or became financially inefficient for many businesses.

The real perk of the defined benefit pension is that your money doesn't get added to a pot and invested. Instead, you pay part of your monthly income in exchange for a monthly income in retirement. Basically, these pensions guarantee you a level of income when you stop working. Each payment you make adds a little bit more on to the total that you will receive each month.

I can look at my teacher's pension and tell you what I will be getting each month when I retire. Yeah, they'll adjust it for inflation, but I can see it. I don't need to wait and see how the stock market performs and then get a rough calculation. I know what I am getting.

The only real downside to this is that there is no big pot of money. You can't choose to withdraw the lot and buy a yacht, for example. Instead, it is designed to replicate the income you received while you were still working.

WORKPLACE PENSIONS

Most people, if they have had a job, will have been offered or even automatically signed up to a workplace pension. This is the most popular pension people have because when they do, not only are they making contributions to it, but their employers are too. It's like free money really.

This is not a different type of pension, but a different way of offering a pension. The pension itself will usually fall into one of the types previously mentioned depending on where you work, and different jobs will offer their pensions through different providers.

Back in my grandparents' generation, you would get a job and stay there for most of your working life. You might pay into that one pension for all the years that you were there. Nowadays nobody does that. The Great Resignation has us switching jobs like underwear and it is the norm to have multiple tiny pension pots all over the place. I'll talk in a bit about what you can do about this.

PERSONAL OR PRIVATE PENSIONS

You don't have to have a job to have a pension. You can have a pension that you have set up on your own, and pay into it yourself. These are commonly used by the self-employed who want to save for their retirement and don't have an employer to set one up for them, but are available to anyone who wants to boost their retirement funds.

They are essentially a wrapper around an investment account that brings you the tax benefits of pensions but also locks your money away until you are in your mid-fifties or later. But depending on who you sign up with you can choose to invest your money in whatever you like. You might decide to pay someone to manage it for you or you might want to look after it yourself. The choice is yours!

Let's Talk Auto-Enrolment

In 2012, auto-enrolment was introduced in the UK. This meant that any employee who met a certain set of criteria would have to be automatically signed up for a workplace pension. Those criteria are:

- You're aged between twenty-two and state pension age.
- You earn at least £10,000 a year.
- You normally work in the UK.[23]

Furthermore, once you are signed up your employer has to make contributions to your pension too. This means that they are paying towards your retirement. I like to think of this as my 'future money'. It's good to treat this as part of your salary that you are deferring because, if you decide to opt out – and you can do this – then you will miss out on those employer contributions too.

Furthermore, the government has set out minimum contributions to pensions that must be made by employers and employees. This works out as 3 per cent of your salary for employers and 5 per cent for you, but there are tax benefits for pensions too. Money that you pay in is entitled to tax relief if you are an income tax payer too, so from a tax perspective it can be advantageous to pay into your pension.

Thanks to the introduction of auto-enrolment, the percentage of people actively paying into a pension has risen from 56 per cent in 2012 to 89 per cent in 2021,[24] which is a huge jump and means that more of us will be better prepared for retirement. If you can afford to stay in your company's pension scheme, then it is likely worth it in the long run.

How to Look after Your Pension

It's time to nurture your pension, baby! This is the good bit. You've got one, or maybe several, and now you get to watch your money do its thing and grow and develop into the pension that is going to support you later in life.

Unfortunately, most people ignore theirs until well into their fifties, when they finally decide they can't be arsed to work any more and then sit there and wonder why they don't have enough to live off. I refuse to let that be you! You are going to take what I am teaching you here and put it into action.

Step 1: Find your pensions

If you have had more than one job since you turned twenty-two, then you probably have more than one pension. If you are anything like the rest of the population, then you probably have no idea who those pensions were with or how much is in them. This is your first task: find out!

Luckily, the government has a tool to help you do this, called the Pension Tracing Service.[25] What you need are your personal details and details of your previous jobs including where you worked and when. With this information, you can find the details of the pension provider that was managing your pension and reach out to them for details on how you can track it.

I know, I know! This sounds like a total slog, but you can do one a month or something if you need to. But remember that this is your money. If it was a bank account full of your cash, I bet you'd be doing everything you could to get your hands on it. Put the same energy into this.

Step 2: Check your investments and the fees

The next step is to look at what your money has been invested into. Are you happy with this? I'll talk more about the types of investments and things like ethical investments in the next chapter, so you can decide what's right for you.

What has the performance been like on those investments, too? Have you seen your money grow or has it just been a steady decline? I am making you do this because I want you to decide if this is somewhere where you want to keep your money – because you could potentially move your money if you wanted to.

Fees are important. What are they charging you for your investments? You might find that there is a fee for just having the pension and then a fee for the fund too. It could be, if these are too high, that they are eating into your capital year on year and your money isn't growing. It could even be declining, meaning you are losing your money.

If you have a defined benefit pension, all you need to do at this stage is check that it is accurate. Have all the payments you made from your salary actually landed in your pension? (Sometimes they do seem to wander, so make sure you check.) And what's your projection looking like?

Step 3: How much pension do you need?

Once you have found all your pensions, you will want to know if you are on track to have enough money to retire and maintain the standard of living that you want. For those with defined benefit pensions, your pension statement should clearly show what you can expect to get when you retire. You should then be able to see, based on your age, whether or not you are on track.

For defined contribution pensions, this will be a bit harder. The thing is, they are investments, so it is hard to predict what will happen with them over the next couple of decades before you retire. Instead, you'll have to use a bit of guesswork – and some handy online calculators.

Money Helper (a website run by the government and the Money and Pensions Service) offers a free pensions calculator (just do a quick google), where you type in all your information and it will give you an estimate of the income you can expect to receive when you retire. Obviously take it with a pinch of salt; life changes and so will your pension, so you need to be prepared for those fluctuations. You never know, it might all turn out better than you expected.

It is all good and well knowing how much you are expecting to get, but will it be enough? Pension Works, a leading independent pensions specialist, recommends that you need about two-thirds of your pre-retirement income to live off when you retire. Therefore, if you are bringing home around £1,800 a month now, then you should be able to achieve the same standard of living on around £1,200 a month when you retire. But I'll let you decide whether you think that's accurate or not.

Step 4: Think about consolidating your pensions

If you are someone who has several pensions floating around in different accounts, then you might be wondering about bringing them all together in one pot. And this might not be a bad idea. But before I go any further, I want to say that pensions can be a tricky business and before you go making any changes you may well want to speak to a financial adviser. In fact, many pension companies will not allow you to move money over a certain amount without consulting a financial adviser first.

What you need to consider are the fees, the costs to move pensions and where you want to put them. You want to make sure that you are not going to lose out here. The last thing you want to do is move your pension to somewhere with poorer performance and even higher fees. This is why I wanted you to do all that research earlier.

Thankfully though, if you do decide to bring all these pensions together, there are lots of great providers that make the whole process easy. They help you move your pensions and keep you updated on the progress. Furthermore, there are now apps and websites that make it easy for you to check in on your pensions and see how they are doing.

Step 5: Check in on your pensions

Pensions do not require daily, weekly or even monthly check-ins. They are designed for the long term and you are going to need to leave them alone and let them do their thing. But equally, you aren't just going to leave them be for the next 40 years and hope the whole thing works itself out.

Every six to twelve months, I want you to load up your pension statement and make sure that everything is going to plan. I want you to make sure that all your payments have gone in and so have all the ones from your employer.

You can have a little look at the impact of the fees and also, if you have a DC pension, make sure that it is growing nicely.

If you change jobs, I want you to make sure that you keep records of your pensions from your previous job, and I want you to get hold of the pensions information from your new job too. You might decide to bring your pension from your previous employer in with your other old consolidated pensions, if you decide that's the right move for you.

Remember that this is your money! As I said in Step 1, if it was a pile of savings in your account you wouldn't just ignore it. You'd check in on it regularly to make sure that everything was okay. Give the same energy to your pensions.

BONUS Step: Increase your contributions

Something you might want to consider is increasing your pension contributions. Again, this shouldn't be done lightly, and you might want to get some expert advice about your personal situation on this one. But if you have looked at your pensions and thought, 'That ain't enough,' then increasing your contributions could be a good way to go.

This could be particularly worth considering if you are employed and your employer is offering to pay more into your pension (up to a limit) if you pay more in too. This way, by agreeing to pay more into your pension yourself you could effectively increase the amount of money that you get out of your employer. Of course, this extra money that you get from them will be going into your pension, so you'll have to wait a few years before you get to see any of it. But still, more money eh?

You might be thinking, 'I can't afford the pension I've already got' and to that I would say, 'Okay'. You don't have to increase your contributions. But I would strongly urge you not to stop contributing to your pension if you can. You are going to need that pension, I promise. So even if all you do for now is the minimum, you'll be so grateful later in life.

State Pension

You might have read everything in this chapter and be thinking that it is all pointless because you'll get a state pension anyway. And while you are not wrong, I do want to dive a little deeper into this and show you exactly what the state is offering you.

Firstly, in order to qualify for any form of state pension you need to have at least ten qualifying years of National Insurance contributions. If you have been working and paying tax, then you will mostly have hit this. To get the full amount you need 35 years' worth of qualifying years, and even this will only entitle you to just over a couple of hundred quid a week.

And yeah, that's not to be sniffed at. But also, is it really enough to live on?

What you are aiming to do when you pay into your workplace pension or your private pension is to top that up so that you can spend your final years doing what you love and not scraping together the pennies to just be able to put your heating on this winter.

The other thing to consider here is that you have to wait until the state retirement age in order to access this pension. For most people reading this book, you are looking at this being at least 68, but there's nothing to stop the government from increasing that. You could well be 70 before you start getting this money.

I'm not sure I wanna wait until I am 70+ to retire.

On the other hand, most of us will be able to access our pensions at 57 years old. That's a lot more like what I had in mind. Even if you just use this money to reduce the amount you work until your state pension kicks in, that's got to be better than slogging away like you are now through your seventh decade on this planet.

To summarise, I am very grateful that the state pension exists and I intend to enjoy it when I get it. But I'm going to save for my retirement like it doesn't exist because I want to be in control of the lifestyle I have in my senior years and I want better for me. And I want better for you too.

Self-Employed Pensions

I gave a deep sigh as I started writing this section, because it kinda breaks my heart just how underprepared the self-employed are for retirement and I think it is going to take a lot of work to change. Therefore, I hope if you are self-employed and you are reading this that you will be the one to buck the trends and go all in on saving for your retirement.

The reality of the situation is that the number of self-employed people regularly paying into a pension fell from 33 per cent in 2005–06 to just 14 per cent in 2014–15 – and I dread to think what has happened over the last decade.[26] What we do know though is that the number of people who are self-employed has increased, and it is because you and I are claiming back our working lives.

You know that I am a big fan of self-employment. Hell, I have been self-employed for six years and I love it.

But bestie! You cannot love all the perks of self-employment and then ignore the fact that perhaps one day you don't want to work because either you are too old, too tired, or you just wanna be able to help out more with your grandkids or jump on a cruise ship and never come back.

Therefore, please please please get a bloody pension!

I've got you covered in the next chapter as I'll explain all the ins and outs of investing, which will help you navigate the whole pension thing too. But the main thing to remember is that when you are self-employed you have complete control over your pension. You get to call the shots and decide how much you pay in and where you put it. You aren't tied to whatever your employer chooses for you. There's a freedom in that.

Furthermore, you can talk to your accountant, if you have one, about paying into your pension in the most tax-efficient way. Regardless of your circumstances, pensions are generally considered good on the tax front, and you should either be able to receive tax relief on your contributions or pay into your pension tax-free.

I hope that whatever your circumstances you'll close off this chapter thinking, 'I need to look after my pension!' Because you really do. They don't look after themselves. Plus, with the right nurturing they can turn into something that will let you live your wildest pensioner dreams!

Chapter Ten

Should You Be Investing?

Yes!

That's the short answer to this question. The longer answer is that if you have a pension you probably already are investing and, as I promised you in the last chapter, you probably want to know how it all works. You're smart! I like you!

Confession time from me to begin with. I didn't actually start investing until I was 30. Now that is probably still quite young given that most people aren't active participants in their investments... well, ever! But if you look into it you'll realise that, even by starting investing at 30, I missed out on some key years to grow and build wealth.

But I'm not completely over the hill on this investment thing, and nor are you. Whatever age you are, you can still experience the benefits of investing.

The thing is that investing is all about making your money do the heavy lifting. You've been working all these years to bring money into your household to pay for the things that you love and your money has just been having a good old time sitting in your bank account. Well unlucky, money! It's time for you to work too.

Back in Chapter Seven, I chatted about how you can use savings accounts with the best interest rates on the market to save towards your short- and medium-term goals. But for those long-term goals, you should really think about investing.

When you invest, you send your money out in the world to go and be productive. This could be in supporting other people's businesses or it could be by providing a loan to the government to help them achieve their goals. Then after 10, 20, 30 or even 40 years, you see what your money has achieved in that time. By sending it in the right direction, you hope that it will come back with so much more than you started with.

Money makes more money.

This is literally the secret to the rich getting richer and, honestly, it is not that complicated.

I remember as a child knowing that investing was a thing, but thought that it was very much *Wolf of Wall Street* and that it was for the few who existed in that world, and let's face it mostly for men. It looked scary, loud and complicated. To help cement this viewpoint in my younger years, I had a boyfriend when I was 17 and he was all into stocks and shares. He never told me how it worked, but went to uni to study finance (dumped me – cheers mate!) and eventually went on to become a stockbroker. I was like, 'Okay, so you have to be a certain type of person then.'

Fortunately, when I turned 30, I thought, 'Enough is enough. It's time that I learned how to invest.'

So that's what I did.

Turns out that it did not take very long, because it is easier to understand than you probably think. And it is so far from the scary, loud and complicated view that I had built up in my head. Instead, it is calm, quiet and easy. I genuinely believe that, even if you have never invested before, you can learn to love it and find joy in the process. You don't even have to be a money nerd like me.

To get you started I want to guide you through some of the terms and underlying principles that you'll need to navigate the world of investing.

One thing before you get into the ins and outs of investing. I want to tell you why you should be considering investing in the first place. Otherwise, you are going to think it ain't worth your time and skip over this chapter.

The answer is compounding returns.

When you invest, the hope is that your money will grow, and for the majority of people this works out. People are investing because they want more than the couple of per cent that is being offered by their savings account. They want to beat inflation and then some. For generations, investing in the stock market has been the go-to vehicle to make that happen.

Let's take a look at some numbers then. Since 1993, if you had invested in an index tracker fund that followed the S&P 500, which are the top 500 companies on the New York Stock Exchange, the average return in that time would have been 10.04 per cent, which adjusted for inflation is 7.32 per cent.[27]

If you had a time machine and went back to 30 years ago and started investing £250 a month, what would you have ended up with? The rough answer is £310,000 ish (you can use an investing calculator to help you out with the detail). But here is the really good part: only £90k of that was money that you put in. Meaning that you would have made £220,000 from your investments.

This is what makes investing so exciting. With even a moderate 7 per cent return (but a good amount of time), you can see some big numbers. And let me reiterate this: time is the key!

Compounding returns need a long period of time to get to work. The longer the better. That's why, when I said I was a late starter to investing at 30, I meant it. The best time to start investing is the day you are born. Thankfully though, the second best time is now. So let's get on with it.

The Basics of Investing

In essence, when you invest you are engaging with the stock market. When you do this, there is a level of risk. We all know this. Your money can go up, or your money can go down. In fact, I can almost guarantee that it will do both at some point on your investing journey. You need to know this before you start because, if you jump into investing and then your money drops a bit and you get scared, your investing journey is going to be a short one.

The nature of investing is that it IS going to go up and down, up and down.

What you are aiming for is bigger ups than downs. Your strategy is going to play a key part here, and I will talk about your different options for this in a bit.

What can you invest in then?

Anything. If you are a homeowner, then you have invested in property. It's just a form of investment that's not floating on the stock market. You might have seen adverts for investing in things like whisky, or, more unusually, art. Some people invest in old cars. There are all sorts of things that can be considered investments. I had a whole stash of Beanie Babies that I bought in the nineties as an investment. That was a poor financial decision, I can tell you that.

What we are dealing with in this book, though, are the types of investments that you can get your hands on via an investing platform, which is typically stuff on the stock market.

STOCKS AND SHARES

These are probably the main ones that you have heard of. If you were to invest in these, you would be buying part of a company. You could have some small amount of ownership over some of your favourite brands. You could buy shares in Amazon or Starbucks or Nike.

When you do this, you can make money in a couple of ways. You might receive dividends, which is when the company decides to distribute some of the profits it has made to its shareholders. The more profitable the company is the more dividends you stand to receive.

Alternatively, you could make money from the increasing value of those stocks. For example, if you had bought shares in Apple 30 years ago you would have seen the values of those shares increase, meaning that, if you sold them now, you'd be selling them for more than you paid for them. Hence, you've made some money.

Generally, stocks and shares are considered one of the riskier types of investments, especially if you are just investing in one or two companies. Your money is then all tied up with the success of those companies.

BONDS

These are different from stocks and shares in that rather than owning part of the company you loan your money to that company instead. This 'company' could be a private business, but more likely it is a government organisation looking to raise funds for a project.

The way you make money on bonds is a little different. You can still try to sell them for more than you paid for them. Same as with stocks. But rather than receiving dividends you get interest payments. Basically, you are paid interest from the organisation that you have loaned money to.

As a result, these are considered less risky investments. Most people think of them as a step up from a savings account. There is an increased risk, as you can still lose money if you sell bonds for less than you paid for them, or if the company defaults on their payments. But that's less likely than with stocks.

FUNDS

The other alternative, and it is a very popular one, is to invest in funds, which are groups of stocks, bonds or a mixture of both, and maybe even some other stuff thrown in for a bit of fun. The real benefit of funds is that you aren't committing your money to any one investment but spreading it out over all sorts of stuff; therefore, if one element goes south, you hope that the rest of the fund will help you weather that storm.

You have a few options when it comes to funds. You can choose either active or passive funds.

Active funds are where you have actual people deciding what to invest your money in. They'll look at how well the investments have been doing and move your money around to where they think they'll get the best return for you.

The opposite of this is a passive fund, where your money gets moved around automatically based on a set of criteria. For example, you could invest in a fund that tracks the FTSE 100. This is a list of the top 100 companies on the London Stock Exchange. What that fund would do is automatically allocate your money across all of those companies. If a company falls off that list, it'll get replaced by another company. And your shares in that company will be sold and you'll buy shares in the new company.

By investing in funds, you are diversifying your portfolio. Meaning that you spread out your money, and consequently reduce your risk.

Plus, there are all sorts of funds to choose from. You can get funds that include just UK stocks, or just US stocks, or a mixture from all over the world. Or you can get funds that only include tech companies or food industries or organisations in the finance and banking sector. If you can't pick, then go for one that includes them all.

Morally Aligned Investing

Before I take you down the route of telling you how you can get started with investing and sorting out your strategy, I want to tell you why I think our generation is amazing.

We care! You care! When you go shopping, you think about sustainability. You want the products that you own to come from ethical sources, and you want to know that the planet is being looked after as well as the people and the creatures that inhabit it.

Even better is that millennials and Gen Z are driving morally aligned investing, with 90 per cent of us interested in ESG investments[28]. ESG stands for Environmental, Social and Governance and it is a label given to companies that are working towards a better future for the planet and its people.

And I love this!

It is like we are saying no to the companies that are

doing bad stuff and refusing to give them our money. And let's face it, that is how change happens in this world. When we vote with our money these companies sit up and listen. They want our cash.

The great news is that investing and pensions are becoming much more accessible and user-friendly. There are apps that allow you to invest wherever you are. You can be sitting on the toilet and decide to invest. Likewise, if you've just heard that a company you are invested in has been polluting a river and this has led to lots of locals becoming ill, then you can sell those shares – from the bus or the train or in the middle of that 'important' Teams call.

This ever-increasing choice and availability means that you can absolutely align your investments with your morals. Whatever they are, and however unique they are.

Let's say that climate change is something you are super passionate about. Well, you could decide that you refuse to invest in oil companies and that you are going to invest your money into those organisations that are looking into renewable energy tech. Perfect!

Or perhaps you are a huge animal lover. You could exclusively invest in companies that refuse to do animal testing and are proactive in fighting for animal rights, and shun any company that isn't on board with that.

Don't want to invest in tobacco companies? Sure! No guns? You can do that! Need your investments Shariah-compliant? That exists too.

Whatever you are passionate about, you can invest accordingly.

The best part is that many investment platforms know that you have strong feelings about where your money goes, and have created funds that include a whole bunch of companies that are aligned with your beliefs too. I would bet good money that, whatever matters to you, there's a fund out there for you.

Make My Money Matter is an organisation that knows the power of your investments, and I am including your pensions in this. They are actively campaigning for more people to move their investments away from fossil fuels and other less desirable companies. One statistic on their website claims that £88 billion of UK pension money is invested in fossil fuel companies. This works out at £3,000 per pension holder, and I expect that it includes your money too.[29]

The message here is that your money is powerful. You have to be an active participant in where that money goes, otherwise it could be working against what you believe. Imagine if instead you invested your money into companies that were doing amazingly wonderful things. Take that £88 billion and do some good with it.

Your Investing Strategy

It is time for you to get to the good part and get investing. You are going to learn how to choose the right account, and the right platform, and then choose your investments.

What I am not going to do though is tell you where exactly to put your money.

I want you to figure out what is right for you, based on the information that I am going to give you in this section. You'll be fully equipped after this to go out there and do the research and pick something that works for you.

Step 1: Choosing your account

First things first: you need to decide what sort of account you want. This is essentially the vessel through which you will do your investing. You'll pop your money in there and then decide where to put it after that. You have a few options:

1. A general investment account (GIA)
   This is the simplest kind of investing account. They are to investing what current accounts are to banking; they are the most basic and every investment platform will offer one.

   The downside is that any investments that you have in one of these accounts will be liable to both dividend and capital gains tax. Therefore, you will need to keep track of what you are buying and selling through this account and, potentially, fill out a self-assessment tax return and pay tax on that money.

   Perks: Widely available.
   Downsides: TAX!

2. Pension
   All pensions are is a form of investment account. You

can pay money into them and invest through them, just like with a GIA. Therefore, you are probably already an investor. You could decide that taking control of your pension is the best first step on your journey as an investor, and it would be a good one.

The main benefit of pensions is that they are a tax-efficient way to invest. You either get tax relief on what you pay in or you can pay in out of your pre-tax income. Plus, if you are employed you get employer contributions too.

There are some limitations to pensions though. Firstly, you have to be in your mid- to late fifties before you can access your money. It literally gets locked away until you are close to what the state believes to be the right age to retire.

Furthermore, apart from a 25 per cent lump sum, the rest of your pension income is taxable. Therefore if you are receiving over the personal tax allowance thresholds you will have to pay some tax on that money.

Perks: Tax-efficient when paying in.

Downsides: Can't access until you are 57 ish and then you might have to pay tax.

3. Stocks and Shares ISA

The third and final option in this list is the marvellous stocks and shares ISA, and you have probably already guessed that I am a big fan of this type of account. Back in Chapter Seven, I shared some information about ISAs in general, so if you have forgotten you may want to go back and revisit that.

More and more investment platforms are offering S&S ISAs, so you will likely find them in most places, particularly if you are dealing with a UK company. The main benefit of this type of account is the tax-freeness. You don't have to pay tax on any money you make on your investments through this type of account. You can just shove your money in there and let it do its thing.

Additionally, you can take this money out whenever you like (which is true of the GIA too, by the way). But this account has the edge because of the tax benefits. The advantage of this is that you could potentially use this money to help you retire much earlier than your late fifties. And that is what lots of people do. They have a pension for their senior years but use their S&S ISA to save towards early retirement.

Perks: Tax-free investments, baby!

Downsides: £20k limit on ISAs.

The reason that I put this as step one is because you need to know what sort of account you want. After all, not all investment platforms offer all the different sorts of accounts. You don't want to sign up for one and then think, 'Oh balls!' because it didn't offer an ISA or something.

On that note, I really do recommend the ISA. Chances are that you already have a pension and you aren't looking for more of the same. You might think about a GIA; but who would choose to pay tax? Take a look at getting a stocks and shares ISA first. If you find that you have more than £20k to invest in a financial year, maybe think about a GIA then. Until then, enjoy not worrying about taxes.

Step 2: Choosing your investment platform

Oh, man! You are so lucky!

Never in the history of ever have there been so many different investing platforms to choose from. There are soooo many, and you get to pick the perfect one for your investing needs.

Maybe you are a traditionalist and you want to go with something well established with a long history in the world of investing. Then you could look at what your bank has to offer or go for one of the big names in the industry, such as Vanguard, Hargreaves Lansdown, A J Bell or Fidelity. (You might not know much about them yet, but they are big names in the UK and across the world.)

Or perhaps you are less bothered about this and instead want ease, convenience, and to keep an eye on your investments wherever you are. Then you'll probably do better with one of the app-based platforms. Of which you have loads of options. You have Dodl by A J Bell, Freetrade, Trading 212, Stake or Wealthify.

What you want to invest in, how you want to invest and how much you have to invest all matter here too. Even though we have yet to tackle these questions together, they still need consideration before you sign up for a platform.

Some platforms are funds only. Of these, some only

offer their own funds and others will offer a selection from a variety of different providers. Some will offer individual stocks and bonds too. Some will even offer more advanced investing options and things like crypto. Some will use a robo-adviser to help you decide what to invest in and others will leave you to make your own decisions. Some will be purely in US dollars and others will be in UK pounds. Some will let you invest with £1, but others will require a £1,000 minimum investment.

Oh and, if these weren't enough questions to be trying to address at the moment, then you also need to think about fees.

Typically there are three main types of fees that you'll need to check before landing on the perfect platform:

1. Platform fee
   This could be a fixed amount like £10 a month, or, more commonly, it will be a percentage. The lower the percentage the better. Some platforms will offer a free service, but give you access to a limited range of things to invest in. Think carefully about what you want to invest in and whether or not that fee is going to be worth it.

2. Trading fees
   Some platforms will charge you either a fixed rate or a percentage to buy or sell your investments. This can make you hesitate when investing and quickly eat into your overall investments. There are also several platforms that don't charge anything for this.

3. FX rate

   If you are buying investments from another country, such as the US, then you will need to convert your English money into dollars to buy it. This means that you might incur foreign exchange (FX) fees, so it is worth checking those too.]

Step 3: Deciding what to invest in

At this point, you have probably decided what account you want to open and what platform you want to open it on. If so, well done! You have made huge progress.

The next step is working out where you are actually going to put your money and, again, you have some options for this. Incoming list. Sorry!

4. Stock picking

   People who stock pick normally know what they are doing because this is a high-risk strategy. It involves doing your research and choosing which company to invest in. It takes time, effort and knowledge – and you could still pick the wrong one and lose all your money.

5. Funds

   You could choose a fund, or even a couple of funds, and stick your money in those. Remember, you could go for an active fund and pay a higher fee but get a human picking for you. Or you could choose the cheaper passive funds. You could choose one that works with your morals. Or you could choose something that looks to invest in as many companies across the world as possible. This would lead to huge diversification and all you'd need to do would be pick one fund and stick your money in there.

6. Target date funds

   These are clever little options that aim to alter your investments to be less risky as you get closer to needing the money. Therefore, if you think you'll need the money in 2050 because that's when you are going to retire, it will start you off with more stocks and then move more to bonds as you get closer to cashing out. You pay a higher fee for this, but it saves you the work.

For most people, I recommend going with the easiest option and either choosing a passive tracker fund that will follow a global index or going with one of these target date options. The former are easy enough to find on most platforms that offer funds, but you might have to shop around for the latter.

The key here is to be lazy with your investments. You are putting in all the effort now so that later you can just sit back and watch your money grow. The good news is that in recent years investors who have gone down the passive investing route have seen better returns than those who opted for an actively managed portfolio.[30]

Seriously, this is yet another area of finance where being lazy is your friend.

Step 4: Deciding how much to invest

This is a tough one. It's a bit of a how long-is-a-piece-of-string situation. The good news though is that, with the range of different platforms that are available now, you can start investing from as little as £1 if you want to.

If you are nervous about investing, then this is the perfect place to start. You can put aside a few quid and just try it out. Watch the money go up and down, try different investments, look at the impact of the fees, and figure out how to navigate your way around the platform. What's the worst that can happen? You lose the £5! That's less than you paid for this book to teach you about how to invest.

Once you have got that all sussed, you then need to think about what you can afford and what you want to achieve with that money. The sweet spot will tick the boxes for both.

Most people who are investing are looking to use their investments to retire early. And I'm talking like super early, in their forties or something. Therefore, these people are prepared to throw all the money that they have into achieving this goal as soon as possible.

Your investing goals and objectives will determine what you feel is a good amount to invest. You don't want to spend all your money investing and leave yourself short on your rent or spend your entire life at home because you have no money for fun. There needs to be a balance.

Working out what you hope to achieve by investing, and when, will give you a target to aim for each month.

Plus, if you catch the investing bug you will likely find yourself looking for ways to make more money and cutting your spending so you can start investing more and more.

You should have the foundations now for starting your investing journey. Take it slow, but go dip your toe. It ain't the scary world that the media would have us believe it is. Rather, it is a powerful tool that is available to us all to grow our wealth and achieve those truly massive goals. Good luck!

Chapter Eleven

The Future of Money?

I want you to cast your mind back all the way to December 2017. What was happening in your world back then? A time before we had even heard of Covid-19 and a time when we were all still reeling from the fact that Brexit was going to happen. Ugh!

But there was something else being talked about, probably for the first time, on the news.

Bitcoin!

Suddenly, this word that we had never heard before had been brought to our attention. There were people out there who were making A LOT of money from this so-called digital currency, and loads of people wanted in.

Now I have to admit that most of this kinda passed me by. I had a two-year-old and a six-month-old baby and I was in a world of sleep deprivation and baby-led weaning that had turned my brain to mush. Back then, I wasn't even a financial educator. Yes, I was interested in money, but I hadn't started writing and teaching about it. I was just curious.

That said, somewhere in my subconscious I knew that

this was going on. Something was happening in the world of money and it looked like it could change things. Maybe even in a big way.

But the whole crypto thing kind of comes in waves.

It will be huge for a while. Look at what happened in 2020 and 2021. Everyone and their dog was buying up all the crypto and everything was going up and up. But come 2022 we were over it again, and I've barely uttered the word 'bitcoin' in the two years since.

But the question is: what happens next?

The introduction of this new world of money has people wondering what it means. Is this going to change the way money works? Is the money in my bank account going to be less valuable? Should I get behind this? Or is it just a fad?

Opinion is very much divided on the answers to all these questions, but in a book that aims to teach you how to manage your money in the modern day I couldn't exactly overlook this. I want you to manage your money successfully now, but I want you to be ready to deal with the money of the future too. So we need to look at crypto.

What Is Crypto?

Big question! I want to start by saying that crypto isn't solely about the money side of things. There's much more to it than that.

Underneath all the hype and the investing and the graphs and the finance bros is a whole new technology called blockchain. This is, simply, a database that is distributed across lots of computers, which means that the data stored in it can't be changed. If it was changed, then it wouldn't match what was on the other computers, so we would know. Of course, I have oversimplified that, but you get the gist.

It is very powerful for a couple of reasons:

1. You have a permanent record. You can look back at this database and see exactly what changes have been made. You can't delete that, so it is there forever.
2. It is decentralised. The blockchain operates on a peer-to-peer system, meaning that it is not controlled by governments or a single organisation but instead by an entire network scattered across the world.

Bitcoin was the first time this new technology was used, and it entered the world back in 2009. No one knows who came up with it, but it has been attributed to someone called Satoshi Nakamoto. That might not be a real person though.

The reason that a currency became the first use of this new technology was because in some ways it works really well. It is secure. You have a track record of the transactions and how the money changed hands. It is global. The money isn't linked to any one country and anyone can access it and use it. It is decentralised. It is not controlled by a government and it requires no third parties like banks to move the money from one person to another. You just do that yourself.

Since the development of this tech and the introduction

of bitcoin to the world, there have been millions more crypto-assets launched into the world. More organisations are looking into how blockchain can be used to improve the systems that already exist, and this has led to new ways to engage in the crypto world.

Smart contracts are one of my favourite ways that blockchain tech is reimagining an old problem. These are basically computer programs that are set up to make something happen. For example, it could be that a company needs more supplies and a smart contract is activated that orders the part and automatically makes payment for it. The record of the transaction is permanent and the movement of the payment is swift.

Another one is NFTs, non-fungible tokens to give them their full name. These have garnered themselves a bad rep, mostly because people bought a load of random digital images thinking they'd be worth something and then all of a sudden they were worthless, or close enough. But NFTs can act as a way of proving ownership. This could be digital art, or it could be a video you posted online or a ticket to an event.

The general consensus among those in the tech industry is that blockchain is here to stay because it is actually quite useful.

What is less certain is what the world of cryptocurrencies will look like. Bitcoin might stay, or it could disappear and may or may not be replaced by something else. The same could be said about all of the current applications of blockchain. Who knows what will last or what might come next?

SHOULD YOU INVEST IN IT?

If you could travel back in time and invest in the internet, would you? I'm guessing that the answer is probably yes. I mean the internet has been a revolutionary invention and the modern world wouldn't exist without it.

But here is the question: how would you invest in the internet?

It is not a company like Apple, Amazon or Meta, where you could buy shares in it and watch them grow over time. It is a thing. A thing that everything else uses. So yes, perhaps you might have invested in one of the companies that uses the internet, like the ones I have listed above. Or perhaps you might have invested in the physical technology that the internet requires, such as phone lines or computers. Or you might have decided to invest in the companies that were working to make it bigger, better and faster, such as the telecom companies themselves.

You could say the same about the AI phenomenon that is unfolding right now. If you were going to invest in that movement, what would you decide to invest in? A company that uses it? The research team? Physical stuff needed to make it happen?

Let's now circle back to how this applies to crypto. Well, I said that blockchain is probably here to stay and it could revolutionise lots of different industries. But investing in it is tricky.

Those who are supporters of the blockchain idea and crypto more generally are investing in it because they believe in the potential. Like I said before, though, we don't quite know what parts are going to stay and what is going to go, so it is all a bit of a risk.

Back in the late 1990s and early 2000s, you might have chucked all your money at the likes of Ask Jeeves, MSN Messenger and Myspace, because they were the biggest things happening on the internet at the time. Smart investing might have seen you make good money on these for a while, but now they barely exist.

Bitcoin could be one of these names. Or it could end up being a huge success. I don't have a crystal ball and neither do you. We won't know the long-term forecast on this one until it is too late to do anything about it.

The whole thing could turn out to be a massive fad, just like the boomers on the internet have been telling us all along.

If, however, you feel like this could turn out to be something huge, then you need to decide what part of it you want to invest in.

How Should You Invest?

You could decide to invest in something that is using this technology and this could be a case for investing in cryptocurrency, such as bitcoin. But there are plenty of companies that are using this technology too, so you don't have to restrict yourself to the only element of crypto you have heard of.

You could support the physical technology that is

needed to run these systems and, for crypto, you would be looking at powerful PCs and their components. Nvidia, for example, has seen a huge rise in their stock price as people turn to bitcoin mining to make some cash. Their high-powered graphics cards have become the go-to for people looking to get involved in the world of crypto.

Alternatively, you could look at the digital systems that people are using to further develop products and services involving blockchains. Ethereum is a good example of this. It is a global decentralised software platform that is powered by blockchain and is considered the platform of choice for developers who are looking to use this technology in new and exciting ways. It also has its own native coin, ether, which is the second most popular cryptocurrency.

There are other platforms out there too. Bitcoin has one and you can build on that if you want. And that's the number one cryptocurrency.

What is the answer to all this then?

Well, you could just ignore it. I'm betting that you didn't invest in the internet either, nor Apple, Amazon, or Meta, and you are still here. You can watch what happens without really worrying too much about the consequences, and just see what this technology may or may not bring into our lives.

Alternatively, you could take the approach of diversifying your portfolio and put a tiny part of your wealth into the industry. Maybe 1 per cent or less, so that if it does all work out then you got involved and maybe you'll make some money but also, if it all goes horribly wrong, then it is only 1 per cent.

Like I have said all along, neither you, I nor anyone else for that matter knows what is going to happen. If you want to dig a bit deeper you could go grab a pile of books from the library, read all the articles online and watch a load of YouTube videos about it. As always when it comes to anything money-related, it's personal!

Is It Going to Change the World?

Whatever happens in the world of cryptocurrency, I think that there's one certainty and that is that money isn't going to stay the same forever.

There has already been a rise in the number of payments that are made using debit and credit cards and, as a result, the number of purchases made using cash has fallen from 54 per cent to 14 per cent in a decade.[31]

On top of this, you have a growing mistrust of banks. In a survey by IT-company GFT, 48 per cent said that they wouldn't trust their bank to help them through a recession and 40 per cent said their bank wasn't meeting their personal needs.[32] People are looking for banks and other finance institutions to do more, to help them, but to also be more innovative in their approaches. I would essay a guess that many of us are still holding a bit of a grudge from the 2008–09 credit crunch.

The landscape of money is already changing.

Cash will likely get used less and less. Hell, my kids

are eight and six and they are using bank cards to buy their sweets from the corner shop. They get their birthday money via bank transfer and their pocket money via direct debit. They only ever use cash if we go to the funfair, and even there most vendors will accept cards to go on the bouncy castle or to buy candyfloss.

Mixed into this is the fast-paced world of fintech, and I love it.

We have seen digital banks like Monzo and Starling drag their high street competitors kicking and screaming into the modern day, with their feature-rich apps that provide a levelling-up for our finances. Plus, there are a million more apps that are helping people pay off debt, get mortgage-free and track their pensions. It's bloody exciting!

I hope that it all continues to change. I want to see what money and finances can do next. I want to see how it can make all of our lives better, easier and more fun.

Do I think that cryptocurrency will have some role in the money of the future? I mean, yeah! Probably! There's already talk of Britcoin, the UK's answer to the whole thing. You just know that's going to be a laugh at the very least.

Things are going to change in the world of finance. That's inevitable. But I can guarantee that nobody quite knows what that will look like ten years from now. So just try to keep up, okay?

Chapter Twelve

It's Not Money, It's You!

It's taken 11 chapters, but I hope you realise now that money moves differently these days. What worked for your parents and your grandparents just doesn't do it any more. They told you that if you worked hard and kept your nose clean then it would all work out all right. But that ain't enough in the current financial climate.

Despite the change in the rulebook, there is one thing that has stayed the same: YOU are in the driver's seat.

You don't have to give up and resign yourself to a life of poor finances and no fun. You don't have to give in to the idea that the economy isn't as good as it was so you'll never get the same financial opportunities as previous generations. You don't have to accept any of that negativity. Because your thoughts and your mindset are down to you.

The many pages that have come before this one have given you the practical tools to take your finances from surviving to thriving in today's society. But the practical skills are only half the story. You need to change your thoughts too. You need to believe that it is possible to be successful, abundant, fulfilled and bloody good at this thing called money.

Thankfully, what we know about money mindset and behavioural finances has come a long way in the last few years and we now know more than ever about how the mind processes money.

And don't go thinking that this is some sort of voodoo hippy nonsense either.

Mindset work has been trialled and tested and seen results that are undeniable. One study conducted by Ramsey Solutions surveyed 10,000 self-made millionaires and found that 97 per cent believed that they could become millionaires even before it was something that was within reach for them.[33] This belief was part of what drove them to look for new ideas and work on their finances until they made that belief a reality.

But it is not all about reaching those dizzy heights of millionaire status. It can be about the small shifts from thinking that you are crap with your budget to feeling confident that you have everything under control. Or feeling like you'll never be able to save enough to knowing that you can save what you need.

What IS Money Mindset Then?

Everyone has a set of underlying thoughts, attitudes and beliefs about how they think money works and how good they think they are at managing it. During our lifetimes we witness those close to us interact with money in a variety of ways, and by reading their reactions we start to form an opinion.

Your money mindset will have formed at some point before you turned seven years old. Whenever I hear that statistic, it shocks me. I can't really remember what I was doing at seven years old, but apparently I had formed a set of belief systems about money that would stick with me into adulthood. I swear at that age I was just playing with Barbies and making my teddies sit in rows while I took a register and played schools. What on Earth could I have known about money at that age?!

Well, it seems that we learn about money from our parents and caregivers. You might have seen your parents struggling with paying the bills, battling with debt or scrambling to get a job. If you did, you probably grew up thinking that making and managing money is HARD WORK and it just makes people sad.

Alternatively, you may have grown up in a house where money was not a concern. There was enough and you didn't go without, so you knew that money was not something worth worrying about too much.

All of these experiences contribute to you forming your money mindset and, while it may feel like you are never gonna shake it off, it is possible to do some reprogramming. You can unlearn the negativity that has been holding you back and replace it with more positive belief systems that support the life that you want to lead.

You should work on this too. Your money mindset is linked to your self-confidence, your self-worth and your self-esteem. If you spend the rest of your life thinking that you suck with money, then you aren't exactly going to be feeling good about yourself. When you work on this, you'll start valuing yourself more, you'll start believing that you are capable of more, and I genuinely believe that you will see the impact in your bank account too.

Scarcity VS Abundance

One of the biggest concepts in the world of money mindset work is that of a scarcity versus an abundance mindset. It says that most people fall into one of two camps: either you think there's not enough money in the world for everyone to have enough – scarcity – or you believe that there is more than enough for everyone and then some – abundance.

It is my personal belief that the majority of the world lives in a scarcity mindset.

If you have ever thought, 'Well we can't all be millionaires' or 'I'll never have enough money!' or 'That's just life – I'll be living pay cheque to pay cheque forever', then you probably have a scarcity mindset. There's no shame in that. We all have those thoughts from time to time when we are chasing after some bigger goal or life feels particularly tough. Just by acknowledging it, you can start to recognise and rewire those thought patterns.

What is the opposite then?

An abundance mindset is when you believe that there is plenty in the world for everyone. It is the quiet confidence of knowing that, whatever financial struggles you have been through in the past, it always worked out in the end. It is knowing that there is more money in the world now than ever before, so it must be coming from somewhere. It is the peace that comes from knowing that you can have what you need without taking from someone else.

Now this isn't me ignoring the fact that income inequality exists, or poverty, or even those shite months when your MOT, boiler service and house insurance all need paying for. It is knowing that solutions for all these problems exist and can be found without taking away from anyone or anything else.

Let me explain something beautiful about money. It circulates the world and does so much good for everyone. When you get paid, I imagine that you will, particularly after reading this book, decide that you are going to maybe save or invest some of it. But the rest you will spend – you will have to spend, as part of keeping yourself alive and enjoying life. Most people will probably see 75 per cent + of their income go back out of their bank account.

Where does that money go?

Well, it will go to banks to pay your mortgage, which will provide them with the money they need to pay their employees' wages. It will go to the supermarkets to buy food, which in turn will help them pay the wages of the people who work there. It'll go to your hairdresser, maybe your cleaner, your bin collector, your kids' nursery and many many more. All of these people will take that money and use it for similar purposes and it will carry on moving.

Money is not a static object. It is fluid. If more money starts flowing into your life, then I imagine that more money will flow out of it too. You'll spend more naturally, then that money will support the other people in your network. Where then is the harm in having more money flowing your way?

How do you make that move from a scarcity mindset to an abundance mindset? Acknowledgement of the problem is a good first step. Seeing this in yourself will help you make adjustments. You catch yourself saying, 'I suck with money!' and wanting to replace that with something that feels more appropriate, like, 'I am working on my money situation!'

Recognise What You Have

Learning to recognise what you already have is a good starting point. As one Forbes article[34] points out, rather than thinking that 'there are no good jobs out there' or 'I don't have enough skills to compete', you can see what you do have. Look at the years of skills you do have, all the work experience in the field, and think about all the other people who you know have been successful in finding the perfect job. It's not about ignoring the bad, it's more about what you choose to focus on. When you focus on the good stuff, then you'll think the world looks a little bit brighter.

See Abundance

When you have been used to living a life of scarcity, it can be hard to feel like there is an abundance of anything. This is why I like playing 'The Abundance Game'. I get my kids in on this too. You know when you see something once and then you start seeing it all the time? It is basically that. You pick something like yellow cars, and then you just try to see how many you can spot. This works great on long car trips, by the way, parents. You can do this with anything – ice cream vans, pink houses, people wearing hats – and you just start to acknowledge that there are a lot of these things everywhere.

Something else I love doing is stating out loud when I see an abundance of something. Like if I am on the beach, I'll say something like, 'Wow! Isn't it amazing how much sand is on this beach?' Yeah, I might sound a bit ridiculous, but honestly the people in my life are used to it now.

Get Abundant Friends

There's that old saying that you are the average of the five people you spend the most time with, so guess what? If you are spending time with people who are miserable Debbie-downers with a scarcity mindset that radiates from their every pore, then you'll find yourself feeling the same way.

Fortunately, the converse is true too. If you hang out with people with an abundance mindset, then you will start to see the world from their perspective. You'll feel more abundant and it will rub off into your own life.

Express Gratitude

This is a hugely powerful tool in all areas of your life. Literally, when you start expressing gratitude for all of the wonderful things in your life, you'll start to have more wonderful things. It's weird but it is true. And it doesn't even matter whether they are just things you hadn't noticed before. The point is that you are seeing them and you are appreciating them.

I like to express gratitude at least once a day. Journaling works well here, and I'll talk more about this later. But some days it is harder than others. If I have had a shockingly bad day, all I want to do is be all, 'This sucks, that sucks, I'm cursed and everyone hates me!' You know the vibe. I'm sure you've had those days too. On these days, I try to be grateful for what I can see, so I'll look around my living room and go, 'I'm grateful for the house plants that bring colour to the room. I'm grateful for the TV for bringing easy entertainment into my life. I'm grateful for the photos on the wall that are packed with family memories.'

Some days you will have loads to be grateful for and the process will be a doddle. This is why it is good to have these moments written down, so that you can come back to them later and soak up all those beautiful moments again.

Retrain Your Mind

While small tweaks and adjustments to your habits can lead to a big mindset shift, sometimes you just want to do something that actually moves the needle a little quicker. It feels good to be proactive and take action on the mindset shift.

For this, many people turn to affirmations, visualisations, books or podcasts that perpetuate these ideas. I love participating in activities that elevate my mood and leave me questioning my thoughts and feelings. There are lots of affirmations on YouTube, apps for visualisation, and a never-ending list of books and podcasts that will help you to restructure your money mindset.

Limiting Beliefs

Now you have the world of scarcity versus abundance sorted in your head, it is time to take your mindset work up a notch. Limiting beliefs are thoughts you have about the world or yourself that stop you from reaching new heights.

I first learned about this concept from Denise Duffield-Thomas in her book *Get Rich, Lucky Bitch!* She talks about how limiting beliefs can show up in all areas of our lives and stop us from making more money. For example, you might think, 'I'm too young to be a manager!' or 'Only skinny people are business owners!' Objectively, all of this is absolute crap! But you might be thinking these things and therefore subconsciously limiting yourself from reaching your full potential.

Imagine going your whole life thinking that you are just a few pounds too heavy to get that promotion. Or that the money that you want is out of reach because you have the 'wrong' accent. It is literally nuts. Yet I'll bet that you are having thoughts like this all the time. How do I know? Because I have them too.

One exercise that Denise encourages her readers to participate in involves writing down all your money memories. You get a notebook and you trawl through every money-related thought or experience you have ever had and write it down. You list all of these experiences. My first list went on for about six sides of A4, and I have done this exercise several times since and have listed more and more stuff.

Once you think you are done, you sit and go through each one and think about how it makes you feel. What are you holding on to about that memory? What did you take away from it? And is that true? Be still and let the emotions bubble up. You might find that you have something to work on as a result. Or you might find that you that you are done with it. Denise recommends that you forgive and let go of these memories. That's it! Say, 'I forgive you!' then move on to the next one.

It is hard for me to give you any real personal examples of memories that came up for me during this exercise because, once I forgave them, I straight-up forgot about them. I literally just moved on.

What I am left with is stuff I am still working on. But that's okay. I can see these thoughts popping up in my day-to-day business and I'm all like, 'Hell no! I don't think like that!' The undoing of these limiting beliefs can take time, but you'll start feeling the results immediately.

You'll feel the small shifts in your self-confidence and self-worth until, eventually, you will look back at how you used to view the world and be shocked at the progress that you have made.

Fear of Success and the Upper Limit Problem

Have you ever found yourself on the brink of achieving something amazing, then something happens that takes the edge off? Maybe you are smashing it at work, but you are arguing with your partner. Or you get a pay rise and then your mortgage goes up. Or you get a tax rebate and then a parking ticket.

Well, Gay Hendricks describes this phenomenon in his book *The Big Leap*, and calls it the Upper Limit Problem, or ULP for short. He says that, when something starts going well in your life, you panic. You get scared of this change and subconsciously start to self-sabotage. You keep yourself small.

The fear of being successful can hold you back. You might be thinking, 'I have lost the plot. Who in their right mind would stop themselves from achieving greater levels of success?'

Me, for one.

When I first launched my money membership site, The Money Nook, I was super excited to join people up and build a community of people who wanted to work on their finance stuff and achieve big things. I threw myself into marketing and promotion because I knew that it would be helpful. Then people started signing up. And I bottled it. I stopped promoting and I stopped talking about it. At the time I couldn't even explain what was going on. I just halted all efforts to get it out into the world.

When I reflect on it now, I can see that I was ULPing. I knew that this was great and that good things were happening and I got scared. I was worried about how I would manage a large community. Would I need to employ someone? Would I make so much money that I'd have to start paying loads of tax? What if it sucked and suddenly I had hundreds of people telling me that?

The fear of dealing with that next level of success was holding me back and the worst part was, I didn't even know it at the time.

This still happens in my life now. There will be moments when things are going great for me and then I see myself starting to put a spanner in the works. The difference now is that I can catch myself in the act and work towards fixing it. The subconscious is becoming increasingly more conscious.

You might want to spend some time thinking about why you might be holding yourself back in your finances. Are you worried about paying more tax? Do you not know what to do with a large amount of savings? Could you be concerned that family and friends might start asking you for help if you had a lot of money?

There are all sorts of reasons why you might be

stopping yourself. Once you uncover them, you can give your head a little wobble and push on to big and better things.

Journaling

Journaling isn't exactly new. Hell, I was writing in a diary (that's a journal) at eight years old, about all the boys I thought were cute at primary school and how I thought they might be into me too. I'm pretty sure that this is a universal experience that has been happening for generations, so why am I about to chat about this?

Journaling is bloody epic!

I discovered this new form of diary writing back in 2017. I had a new baby and a head full of ideas about the business that I wanted to create. With only a newborn and a two-year-old for company most of the time, I needed an outlet for all these thoughts in my head.

Enter the journal.

There is so much power in being able to take the noise in your head and put it into one single stream of thoughts. It helps you to piece together all the randomness and turn it into something more manageable. Over the years I have tried various strategies for my journaling, including using different prompts, goal setting, gratitude and planning my day. All have helped me to varying degrees and I recommend that you try whatever you can get your hands on too.

When it comes to your finances, journaling can help you unpack those limiting beliefs, help you reflect on your mindset, and also act as a way to track your progress on your journey to financial security.

As a business owner, my journal has been invaluable for putting down on paper my ideas around making money and the ways that I want to implement this. It has further served as a way to showcase the progress that I have made along the way. When I look back to 2017–18 I can see that my business was born out of nothing; and now it makes more than enough for me and my family to live on and then some. This was way beyond my wildest dreams when I first loaded up that blogging website.

You can use it to write out your goals every day to ensure that they are kept front of mind. Plus, you can set mini goals for the day or week ahead, to keep you on track and moving forward.

You could write out any challenges you are facing. Sometimes the mere act of writing them down can help you see a solution that wasn't immediately apparent. Even if it doesn't come immediately, it can help you process the varying components at play and remove some of the emotions that might be clouding your judgement.

My journal has even helped me realise when I'm being an idiot. There have been times when I am obsessing over something that seems like the end of the world. As soon as I put it on paper, it seems so trivial and insignificant that I have to laugh at myself.

If you are sceptical about journaling, then I recommend that you just give it a go. Even after a couple of weeks, you will see the impact that it has across all areas of your life, not just your finances.

But if you want to focus on one thing to start with, then your money seems like a good one. Write every day, but only about your finances, and see if it helps you see things a little differently.

Lucky Thinking

Are you a lucky person or an unlucky one?

It turns out that your thoughts on this can actually impact how lucky you are. If you think that you are a lucky person, you will probably find that you are luckier. Whereas if you think you are unlucky, then you will get all the bad stuff flooding your way.

This is confirmation bias at work.

Confirmation bias means that you are more likely to look for things that support an opinion that you have. If you believe that the world is full of people in blue coats, then you will automatically look for the people in blue coats to support your theory. It doesn't necessarily mean that there are any more people with blue coats in your world; it's more that your brain is wired to see them more.

How would you see the world if you thought you were the luckiest person in it?

Imagine you started to believe you were the luckiest person in the world. Your brain would automatically start to look for evidence to support this viewpoint. Maybe you'd start winning more, or at least notice that you were winning more. Even little things like getting a parking space right outside the supermarket would feel like a win.

And let's say you don't believe that. You spend your

life thinking that you are super unlucky. Then you would train yourself to find reasons to support that belief. That sounds blooming miserable if you ask me. Focusing on the negative all the time and thinking that you are unlucky. Nah, that ain't the one.

You get to choose. It might take time to switch up your perspective, but it is worth the effort. Decide now that tomorrow you are going to wake up the luckiest person in the world. Remind yourself of this before you go to bed and first thing in the morning. See if your life changes.

Income Tracking

The rest of this book has been packed with super practical tips about how to manage your money. Then I spring this chapter on you with all the psychology and mind-work stuff. It's a bit of a change of tone, I agree.

Therefore, I thought I would wind up with something practical that you can do to help you feel more abundant and to see the truth of the money that you have in your life. That is income tracking!

Throughout this book, I have encouraged you to keep an eye on your spending, your savings, your investments and your pensions. But rarely do we think about how much money comes our way. Before you start, yes I know that you have been checking your payslips and making sure that you've been paid correctly. What I am talking about is all the other money. And yes I am convinced that there is other money coming into your life.

As a business owner, I get bits and pieces of money

showing up in my life and my business account pretty much daily. But even in my personal life, I find that money shows up in unusual ways too. I know this because I keep an income tracker.

It is a simple spreadsheet where I record the date, the amount and where the money came from, and I update it every day. It means I can see money coming to me from all sorts of places. I get little refunds here and there, I get money for birthdays and Christmas, people randomly pay me back for stuff that I had forgotten about, I get payouts from cashback apps, and the list goes on and on.

I also track free stuff, although I put this on a different spreadsheet to ensure that I know the difference. These can be discounts I receive thanks to vouchers, loyalty points, buy-one-get-one-free deals or things that people have randomly given me. Again, this seems to happen all the time. The value of these items can be significant, too.

By tracking this, I can see that I have a lot more money flowing into my life than first meets the eye. It adds evidence to that feeling of abundance, confirms that I am luckier than I think and, what's more, inspires me to find money in more places.

I encourage you to try this for a month. Record every penny you find on the street, discount code you use and payment into your bank account. By the end of the month, I am convinced, you will feel a lot richer than you do now.

Mindset work has come a long way in the last three decades. When I was a kid, no one had ever heard of it, and now here we are talking about how you can unpick your old, and possibly even inherited, thought patterns to make even bigger leaps in your finances.

You may feel that the practical tips in the previous chapters far outweigh the psychological strategies and concepts that I have presented to you here. But you are wrong!

You will always struggle with managing your money if you believe that you are bad with money. You will always feel poor if you believe that you are poor. You will never be rich if you believe that people like you aren't destined to be rich.

Unless you take control of YOUR beliefs around money, you will perpetuate those thought cycles forever. And if you need one thing to be grateful about to kick-start your journey, let it be that you have access to this wisdom. You've got one up on your ancestors in that regard.

Conclusion: What to Do Now?

I always get nervous when I reach the end of a book like this. I'm all like, 'Don't leave me, I still need you!' But this is the part where you have to do the work. I'm sorry. But if all you do is read this book and then carry on with your life as before, then nothing will actually change. But you are ready. You've got everything you need now to navigate the modern-day financial landscape. On your terms. Without any of those lingering viewpoints from your mum, dad, Great-Aunt Sue, Nana Mags, or anyone else for that matter.

But before you go I want to give you a few last-minute pointers to steer you in the right direction. One last little pep talk if you please.

Focus On What You Want

The noise of the world can be deafening. Everyone has an opinion, every business wants to sell you something and every thought you have is out to sabotage you.

I promise you that the world gets a lot quieter when you get clear on what you want and focus on making that happen. It's like the planets align and stars come together, and all the work you are putting in suddenly shows up as progress.

Until you know this, you are in a constant state of fighting. The deep desires that you have will be fighting to come out, and you'll be spending your life subconsciously suppressing them in order to make someone else happy.

Work on what you want first. Design your life according to your goals and dreams and then get your finances in alignment with that. Build a career that brings you fulfilment and you'll happily move up that ladder. Save for the things that are going to bring you joy, and the money will flow into your accounts. Plan the retirement of your dreams, and the urge to build your pension up will come automatically.

None of this is magic.

It is about what lights you up. When you find that in all areas of your life, things get easier. You can only get to this place when you know what you truly want from it all, though. Take the time on this. It is worth every second.

Be Flexible

This book is like an MOT. I can only promise that it all holds true at the moment of publication. The thing is that the world of finance is constantly changing and, just as what held true for our parents doesn't work for us, chances are what works for us won't work for our kids.

The message here is that flexibility is needed.

I remember when my eldest daughter was born, I had this app called Wonder Weeks and it would tell me when she was going through some huge developmental leap and that I should expect her to be extra cranky at that point. It only went up to 18 months though, and I was devastated at the time, thinking, 'How will know when she's going to be cranky next?' I expressed this opinion to a veteran mum, and her response was 'After eighteen months, you will know that there's always some reason for them to be cranky, so you just shut up and get on with it.' And she was right.

I hope that you see this book kinda like that app. I hope that it has navigated you through this period of your life, but also set you up to know that you need to be flexible if you want to navigate the next stage. I can't tell you what that next stage will be, but I can tell you that the change is inevitable and you'll need to be proactive if you want to continue to thrive.

There will be new types of apps that help you save and invest. There will be developments in bank accounts that will get you more features to manage your money. There will be changes to taxes and benefits that will change the amount of money that you have coming in. And there will be things that I cannot predict because they are so new and innovative that they will blow my mind.

But you know now that there are benefits to using all

of these things. You have adapted to the world we live in now, so you can adapt and adapt again. You don't need another book in ten years to tell you how to manage your money then, because you've got this. Keep half an eye on the changes and do a bit of research. You'll figure it out.

Buffer the Noise

As you begin your journey to better finances, you will hear a lot of people try to tell you something different. Their way of doing things. They'll tell you that what they did worked really well for them. And you know what, it probably did. But they're not you and their circumstances are very different to yours.

It is important to remember that personal finance is... personal.

You have to make your own choices and decisions that are best for you. And while you can speak to a financial adviser to help make some of these steps, you ultimately need to retain the ownership. Even if this person is best placed to give you good advice, I want you to question it all.

You are going to have friends who have gone all in on Bitcoin and will wax lyrical about why you should do the same. Your parents will tell you that buying a house is the best investment because they made loads of money on it. And some bloke at your office will tell you how you should go for this job that has come up because it would be perfect for you.

Listen to all of it. Be polite. Then quietly do your own research. Hopefully, this book will help you come to your own conclusions about how each of these opportunities may fit into your life or not. But sometimes you might need to dig a little deeper. There are many books, podcasts, articles and YouTube videos that will help you work out what is right for you.

And if that doesn't work, then just block out the noise. You can smile and nod, but let it go in one ear and out the other. You don't need their advice. You are more than capable of managing this on your own now.

Forge Your Own Path

Being different can be a real challenge. I should know. In my family, I have always been the one who wanted to do life contrary to everyone else. I think on a subconscious level I was doing it on purpose. Testing the boundaries to see how far they would go.

This meant that I caused a little friction.

My family have despaired many times as I told them of my next big idea. You should have seen them when I told them I was taking their grandbabies on a trip around the world.

But the friction, however distressing at the time, was still worth it. I wouldn't change any of it. I needed to do things my own way to feel like they were my decision. To feel like I was in control.

And yes, it hasn't always turned out the way I had

wanted to. Things happen. (Hello, Covid-19 you ruinous friend!). But pressing ahead with what felt right for me has pretty much always turned out to be the perfect decision.

So don't be afraid of making choices that might disappoint people. The worst thing that you can do in life is to disappoint yourself, and avoiding disappointing others is a surefire way to achieve that.

Therefore, if you wanna buy the house, buy the house. If you wanna sell up and live on a beach in Bali, then sell up and live on a beach in Bali. If you wanna go for that big promotion, then go for that big promotion. But if you wanna quit and start that brownies delivery business, then go bloody do that.

There's often one person in a family who future generations look to as being the one who changed it all. The one who paved the way for everyone who came after. You could be that person!

Don't Forget to Nurture Your Finances

A book about money wouldn't be truly complete without a reminder to look after your finances. This is literally the entire point of this book, so if you missed that message then maybe you need a reread.

I don't want you to be obsessed with money. That's not the point. It is a tool that helps you achieve all those amazing things that you have been dreaming of doing. It is not the dream itself.

Think of your money as a house plant. It can bring you so much joy, but it shouldn't take up all your energy to make it thrive. It just needs a check-in and a bit of water every once in a while.

But yeah, I do want you to check in on it. Do your budget, keep an eye on your spending, stick some money in your savings and investments, and don't neglect your pensions. If you can, have a little look in on your bank accounts once a week, and everything else every few months, then you can pat yourself on the back and consider it a job well done.

The rest of the time?

I want you to wallow in the peace that comes with financial security. I want you to make memories on that holiday that you have been saving for. I want you to sleep soundly knowing that you have an emergency fund and a retirement plan.

The world of money has changed massively in the last 50 years, but ultimately we all want money and success for the same reason – to help us live our most fulfilled lives. My hope is that you go and do exactly that.

Endnotes

One

1 https://www.swanlowpark.co.uk/savings-interest-annual
2 https://www.officialdata.org/us/stocks/s-p-500/2000?amount=100&endYear=2020
3 https://www.statista.com/topics/8518/digital-learning-in-the-uk/#topicHeader__wrapper
4 https://jobdescription-library.com/remote-working-statistics-uk
5 https://home.kpmg/uk/en/home/media/press-releases/2022/02/uk-fintech-investment-soars-to-37-billion-in-2021.html

Two

6 https://www.shepherdsfriendly.co.uk/resources/savings-goal-will-help-you-save
7 https://www.canr.msu.edu/news/achieving_your_goals_an_evidence_based_approach#:~:text=The%20results%20of%20the%20study,43%20percent%20of%20goals%20achieved.
8 https://www.lyondellbasell.com/4aeca6/globalassets/sustainability/lifebeats/advancing-health/life/goals/newdirectioningoalsetting_locke-et-al..pdf

9 https://onlinelibrary.wiley.com/doi/abs/10.1111/j.1744-6570.1978.tb00449.x

Four

10 https://options2040.co.uk/public-opinion-and-taxation-the-surprising-reality

11 https://commonslibrary.parliament.uk/research-briefings/cbp-8513

12 https://www.gov.uk/government/statistics/annual-savings-statistics-2023/commentary-for-annual-savings-statistics-june-2023#:~:text=Chart%2010%3A%20Proportion%20of%20population,of%20adults%20respectively%2C%20had%20ISAs%20

Five

13 https://www.ons.gov.uk/peoplepopulationandcommunity/personalandhouseholdfinances/incomeandwealth/articles/incomespendingandwealthhowdoyoucompare/2022-03-09

14 https://www.statista.com/statistics/261827/leading-media-companies-worldwide/#:~:text=Leading%20media%20owners%20worldwide%202022%2C%20by%20ad%20revenue&text=In%202022%2C%20Google%20was%20the,spot%20in%20the%20global%20ranking

Six

15 https://staffprofiles.bournemouth.ac.uk/display/report/158853

Seven

16 https://www.gov.uk/individual-savings-accounts/how-isas-work
17 https://www.gov.uk/apply-tax-free-interest-on-savings
18 https://www.gov.uk/lifetime-isa
19 https://citywire.com/new-model-adviser/news/the-unloved-innovative-finance-isa-is-the-wrong-home-for-ltafs/a2431189

Eight

20 https://moneyadvisor.co.uk/average-debt-uk/#:~:text=-Total%20debt%20in%20the%20UK,mortgages%2C%20stood%20at%20%C2%A365%2C756
21 https://moneyadvisor.co.uk/average-debt-uk/#:~:text=-Total%20debt%20in%20the%20UK,mortgages%2C%20stood%20at%20%C2%A365%2C756

Nine

22 https://www.legalandgeneral.com/retirement/pensions/pensions-explained
23 https://www.gov.uk/workplace-pensions/joining-a-workplace-pension#:~:text=Your%20employer%20must%20automatically%20enrol,least%20%C2%A310%2C000%20per%20year
24 https://www.gov.uk/government/statistics/ten-years-of-automatic-enrolment-in-workplace-pensions/ten-years-of-automatic-enrolment-in-workplace-pensions-statistics-and-analysis
25 https://www.gov.uk/find-pension-contact-details
26 https://ifs.org.uk/publications/trends-pension-saving-among-long-term-self-employed

Ten

27 https://tradethatswing.com/average-historical-stock-market-returns-for-sp-500-5-year-up-to-150-year-averages/#:~:text=Stock%20Market%20Average%20Yearly%20Return%20for%20the%20Last%2030%20Years,including%20dividends)%20is%207.32%25

28 https://www.nasdaq.com/articles/how-millennials-and-gen-z-are-driving-growth-behind-esg

29 https://makemymoneymatter.co.uk/oblivian

30 https://www.fool.com/investing/how-to-invest/active-vs-passive-investing

Eleven

31 https://www.ukfinance.org.uk/news-and-insight/press-release/half-all-payments-now-made-using-debit-cards#:~:text=The%20total%20number%20of%20cash,payments%20were%20made%20with%20cash

32 https://www.emarketer.com/content/almost-half-of-uk-banking-customers-don-t-trust-their-bank-help-them-through-recession

Twelve

33 https://www.ramseysolutions.com/budgeting/understanding-your-money-mindset

34 ttps://www.forbes.com/sites/carolinecastrillon/2020/07/12/5-ways-to-go-from-a-scarcity-to-abundance-mindset/?sh=6061a11197dc

Bedford Square Publishers is an independent publisher of fiction and non-fiction, founded in 2022 in the historic streets of Bedford Square London and the sea mist shrouded green of Bedford Square Brighton.

Our goal is to discover irresistible stories and voices that illuminate our world.

We are passionate about connecting our authors to readers across the globe and our independence allows us to do this in original and nimble ways.

The team at Bedford Square Publishers has years of experience and we aim to use that knowledge and creative insight, alongside evolving technology, to reach the right readers for our books. From the ones who read a lot, to the ones who don't consider themselves readers, we aim to find those who will love our books and talk about them as much as we do.

We are hunting for vital new voices from all backgrounds – with books that take the reader to new places and transform perceptions of the world we live in.

Follow us on social media for the latest Bedford Square Publishers news.

@bedsqpublishers
facebook.com/bedfordsq.publishers/
@bedfordsq.publishers

https://bedfordsquarepublishers.co.uk/